CULTURES OF THE WORLD

MALDIVES

954.97 NgCheong-Lum

Roseline NgCheong-Lum

MARSHALL CAVENDISH
New York • London • Sydney

Reference edition published 2001 by
Marshall Cavendish Corporation
99 White Plains Road
Tarrytown
New York 10591

Originated and designed by
Times Books International, an imprint of
Times Media Private Limited, a member of the
Times Publishing Group

Printed in Malaysia

Library of Congress Cataloging-in-Publication Data:

NgCheong-Lum, Roseline, 1962–
    Maldives / Roseline NgCheong-Lum.
      p. cm. — (Cultures of the world)
    Includes bibliographical references and index.
    ISBN 0-7614-1157-7
    1. Maldives—Juvenile literature. [1. Maldives.]   I. Title.
II. Series.
DS349.9.M34 N45 2001
954.97—dc21
                        00-037923
                        CIP
                        AC

INTRODUCTION

RISING OUT OF THE INDIAN OCEAN like a precious necklace, Maldives has always fascinated travelers. Called "flower of the Indies" by Marco Polo and "one of the wonders of the world" by 14th century traveler Mohammed Ibn Batuta, the archipelago used to draw traders shuttling between East and West. The traders stopped for fresh supplies and cowry shells, which were the major form of currency then. Today Maldives attracts travelers in search of peace and tranquility.

For the islanders, however, life is hardly a holiday. Theirs is a harsh life: hours spent at sea fishing or in gardens coaxing the soil to grow some vegetables. But, with their steadfast Muslim faith, they face every day with renewed hope and energy.

With global warming causing sea levels to rise, many of the Maldives islands could become submerged in this century. Maldives is doing its best to educate the rest of the world on the perils of pollution since its destiny depends on finding a solution.

CONTENTS

A fisherman showing off his catch.

4

CONTENTS

A Maldivian man in traditional costume.

GEOGRAPHY

MALDIVES IS A CHAIN of small coral islands in the Indian Ocean. The country's name comes from the ancient Sanskrit language and means "garland of islands." Scattered over an area of 34,750 square miles (90,003 square km) in the Indian Ocean, the 1,190 small tropical islands only add up to 115 square miles (298 square km). Maldives is unique in that the sea forms 99.669% of its territory.

Maldives appears in the *Guinness Book of Records* as the flattest country in the world. No island is higher than 7 feet (2 m) above sea level. The islands have no hills or rivers. Only about 200 islands are inhabited.

The Maldivian archipelago lies about 375 miles (600 km) south of India. But the people have more affinity with Sri Lanka, which is 400 miles (644 km) to the east. Until recently, the only way to get to Maldives was via Sri Lanka.

Left: **Boys returning from collecting corals.**

Opposite: **Sunset in beautiful Maldives.**

THE MALDIVIAN ARCHIPELAGO

The archipelago consists of 26 atolls, each one formed by a coral reef. For administrative purposes, however, the government recognizes only 19 of them. In the middle of each atoll is a lagoon. Islands rise from the outer reef and are protected by their own reef. Deep channels in the reef allow boats to move from one atoll to the other. Each atoll consists of about five to 10 inhabited islands and 20 to 60 uninhabited ones. All 19 official atolls have both an administrative as well as a traditional name. In addition the government uses the letters of the Maldivian alphabet to refer to them.

Although there are officially 1,190 islands, this number can change as islands and sandbanks appear and disappear with the tides.

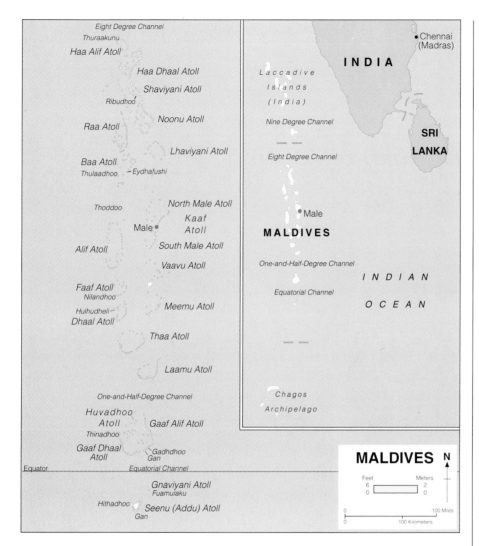

MALE

The most important atoll in Maldives is Male ("MÄ-lé") Atoll. Consisting of North and South Male atolls, it lies halfway down the archipelago. The atoll has 105 uninhabited and 12 inhabited islands. Male, the capital, is on the southern tip of North Male Atoll. Next to it is Hulule, the country's international airport, which was created by flattening an entire island. Male Atoll is the political and commercial hub of the country. Male and the other central atolls support most of the Maldivian population.

One of the largest atolls in the world is Huvadhoo, which lies just above the equator. Its lagoon covers an area of 864 square miles (2,238 square km).

THE NORTHERN ATOLLS

The northern atolls are located near India, and the Indian influence is stronger here. Islands in the northern atolls are closer together, and communication between them is easy. They are least touched by tourism and seem rather remote from the center of activity in Male. Northern atolls are frequently struck by heavy storms. The northernmost inhabited island of Maldives is Thuraakunu in Haa Alif Atoll.

THE SOUTHERN ATOLLS

The southern atolls are separated from the central atolls by the One-and-a-Half-Degree Channel, the broadest and most dangerous stretch of water in Maldives. The channel gets its name from its location, one and a half degrees north of the equator. The southern atolls are isolated from Male, and an unsuccessful secession movement was active in the 1960s. The southern atolls are closer to Sri Lanka, and the inhabitants are different from the rest of the Maldivian population. One of the most well-known southern islands is Gan, which served as a British military base from World War II until 1976. Fuamulaku Island is also an atoll and is the largest island in Maldives.

ATOLL FORMATION

The Maldive islands lie on an underwater volcanic mountain ridge. The atolls are formed when coral growth produces a fringing reef around each volcanic landmass. As the reef grows taller, the land subsides until the volcano disappears completely. Only the reef is left, encircling a lagoon of water where the volcano used to be. This reef continues to grow, and the higher parts eventually become islands.

An atoll is usually oval in shape, with most of the islands located on the outer edges of the reef where coral growth is more vigorous. Some atolls also have islands inside the lagoon, but these tend to be smaller. Reeftop atolls have no interior lagoon, but are composed of a single island covering most of the reef platform.

The composition of each atoll can be altered by ocean currents, storms, or monsoonal changes. Erosion causes many islands to change their shape and size. In some drastic cases, the whole island vanishes into the ocean. On the other hand, whole islands can appear from nowhere after a storm. The islands of Aahura and Udhafushi were formed during storms that hit Maldives in 1955 and 1987 respectively.

Aerial view of atolls.

THAT SINKING FEELING

The greatest threat to Maldives in the next few decades comes from global warming. As industrialized nations emit more noxious gases into the atmosphere, the earth warms up in what is called the "greenhouse effect." This leads polar ice caps to melt and sea levels to rise. Even a slight rise will be catastrophic for Maldives since all the islands are less than 7 feet (2 m) in height. In addition most islands are cup-shaped with a low center.

Scientists predict that sea levels could rise by as much as 15 inches (38 cm) in the next 40 years. The slightest storm could wash away some of the low islands. Some islands, like Male, are already sinking. Even if the islands do not actually sink, they have become more vulnerable to climatic conditions such as El Niño. More frequent storms have been observed in the Indian Ocean, and surging tides pose a definite threat to the islands.

Optimists think that Maldives will not sink because the coral reefs surrounding the archipelago are constantly growing so that the islands will rise as sea levels rise. However the reefs are not growing as fast as the sea is rising, and it is feared that the whole archipelago will be completely submerged in 70 years' time.

Unfortunately for the Maldivians, there is nothing much they can do on their own to stop global warming. It takes a concerted effort from the world's industrialized nations to change their habits and to switch to more ecologically friendly methods of production. With this in mind, the Maldivian president, Maumoon Abdul Gayoom, has traveled tirelessly around the globe to raise awareness of the plight of his country.

CLIMATE

As Maldives is in the tropics, there is little variation in temperature throughout the year. The weather is hot and humid most of the time, with daytime highs of 86°F (30°C) dropping to 75°F (24°C) at night. Sea breezes keep the air moving and help to temper the humidity.

The year is divided into two monsoon periods. The northeast monsoon lasts from December to March; these are the drier months of the year. The southwest monsoon from May to November brings strong winds and storms. In May 1991 tidal waves resulting from violent monsoon winds swept away thousands of houses and flooded large areas. The damage was estimated at $30 million.

The average annual rainfall is 84 inches (213 cm), with the south receiving more rain than the north.

The Male International Airport on Hulule Island. Most visitors come to Maldives by air.

AN ISLAND CAPITAL

The capital of Maldives is an entire island. Male has been the cultural, political, and business center of Maldives throughout its history. The island is small, only 1.2 miles (2 km) long and 0.62 miles (1 km) wide. With a permanent population of 65,000 and thousands of daily visitors, it is one of the most densely populated places in the world. Land reclamation has increased the size of the island considerably, but it still faces great population pressure.

Male is divided into four districts: Henveiru, Maafanu, Machchangolhi, and Galolhu. Henveiru in the northeast overlooks the harbor. It is a rather wealthy neighborhood, with government offices and elaborate villas lining Marine Drive, the main street of the island. Maafanu covers the northwestern end of the island. It houses the Presidential Palace, some foreign embassies, and most of Male's hotels. Situated in the south of the island, Machchangolhi contains Male's main shopping area. Galolhu, in central Male, is where most residents live.

Male's skyline is dominated by the three-story Islamic Center. Opened in 1984, this huge golden-domed complex with 133 minarets houses the Grand Mosque, an Islamic library, a conference hall, and a number of classrooms. Many other mosques are dotted around Male, with the most significant being the Friday Mosque. Built in 1656, it contains intricate carvings and the tombs of ancient Maldivian heroes.

As the country is rapidly developing, Male is constantly changing. Many buildings are torn down to make way for taller ones. Land reclamation goes on in the south and west, and the breakwaters prevent the northern area from being washed away in a storm.

FLORA AND FAUNA

Maldivian soil is quite poor and does not support much vegetation. There are altogether 600 plant species, of which half are cultivated. One interesting feature of Maldivian flora is that almost all the common native species are identical to those of Pacific coral islands. The most common tree is the coconut palm, the national tree of Maldives. Breadfruit, almond, screwpine, casuarina, and banyan trees can be found on the larger islands. Many tropical flowers grow in profusion. Bougainvillea, frangipani, and hibiscus turn the gardens and parks into colorful and scented havens. The national flower of Maldives is the pink rose, which is not native to the tropics.

Wildlife is also limited in Maldives. Small animals and insects make up the land fauna. The most conspicuous animal is the flying fox, a large type of bat. Cats, chickens, and goats are the only domestic animals. There are no dogs in Maldives because the Islamic faith of the population prohibits any contact with the animal. Insects and reptiles include butterflies, scorpions, wasps, lizards, and turtles.

Birds such as the heron *(above)* **are plentiful, with more than 100 species of birds resident in Maldives.**

The marine life in Maldives is very rich, consisting of many fish species and rare corals.

MARINE LIFE

The waters around Maldives teem with marine life. More than 200 types of coral live on the reefs surrounding the atolls. In the sandy lagoons the corals are small and delicate. On the reef edge, where sunlight is less intense and currents are stronger, they are large and robust. Coral colonies come in all shapes and sizes, forming fans, leaves, columns, arches, and caves. Most of them are very colorful.

The most common fish in Maldivian waters is the parrotfish. Brightly colored, it has a beak and swims as if flapping wings. Other fascinating fish include clown fish, butterfly fish, angelfish, and triggerfish. In the lower depths live sharks, tuna, barracuda, rays, and eels. The whale shark is the largest fish in the world. Dolphins, especially the dark gray bottlenose dolphin, are also abundant.

Among the endangered marine species is the giant leatherback turtle. Four species of turtle nest in Maldives: green, olive ridley, hawksbill, and loggerhead. The hawksbill used to be plentiful in Maldives, but numbers have declined due to hunting.

More than 5,000 species of shells are found on the reefs. Maldives is best known for cowry shells. For many centuries the humble cowry was the most valuable product of Maldives. It was used as currency by countries bordering the Indian Ocean.

THE ALL-PURPOSE COCONUT TREE

The coconut palm is truly the tree of life in Maldives. The islanders have found a use for every part of the tree, from the fruit to the trunk and leaves. The coconut provides food with its milk and flesh. The milk of the *kurumba* ("KOO-room-bah") or young coconut makes a refreshing drink. It is also used in cooking. The sweet and tender flesh goes into curries and cakes. The husk is turned into coir and rope. The sap is tapped from the stalk at the crown of the palm and made into a drink. When boiled, it becomes a type of syrup. Coconut oil is extracted from the ripe coconuts.

Coconut fronds are woven to make roofs, mats, and walls. The trunks are made into boats and are used to make houses and furniture. Anything left over is burned as fuel.

HISTORY

MALDIVES' EARLY HISTORY is shrouded in mystery. According to one legend, Sinhalese women were the first inhabitants of the islands called Mahiladipa or "the islands of women." The friendly women welcomed travelers and bore their children. It is probable that the first settlers arrived from Sri Lanka and India before 500 B.C. However, the islands were well known to seafarers as early as 2,000 B.C. Maldives was an important stop on trading routes between East and West, and Egyptians, Phoenicians, Romans, Arabs, and Indians all called at the islands at one time or another. Here they exchanged foodstuff and spices for cowry shells, the money used by the ancient people of the Middle East and India.

According to ethnologist and author Thor Heyerdahl, a mythical people called Redin were the first to settle in Maldives. Not much is known about them except that they were light-skinned giants who worshiped the sun. In 500 B.C., they were either chased away or became assimilated with the Indians and Sinhalese who came to the islands. Maldives was then ruled by a series of Buddhist kings and queens whose history is now mixed with legend.

Above: **A representation of a sun-worshiping king on his throne.**

Opposite: **A memorial built in Gan to commemorate the soldiers in the Indian regiments, such as the 13th Frontier Force Rifles, who died protecting Maldives.**

CONVERSION TO ISLAM

Recorded history in Maldives begins with the arrival of Islam in A.D. 1153. According to Mohammed Ibn Batuta, a Moroccan traveler who visited the islands in the 14th century, a sea monster used to terrorize the people, demanding the sacrifice of a virgin girl once a month. In 1153

The ancient shrine of Abul Barakaath Yusuf Al Barbary.

a Muslim visitor, Abul Barakaath Yusuf Al Barbary, decided to take the place of the chosen girl. He chanted Koranic verses all night, and the monster was never seen again. After witnessing this miracle, the Maldivian ruler immediately converted to Islam, taking the name of Sultan Mohammed Ibn Abdulla. He decreed Islam to be the sole religion of the whole country. It took almost 60 years before all the islands converted to the new religion. Sultan Mohammed Ibn Abdulla founded the Malei Dynasty, which would rule the country for 169 years, but he himself disappeared in 1166 on a pilgrimage to Mecca.

Quaint as the story of the conversion may be, it was certainly for political motives that the Buddhist king of Maldives became Muslim. In the 12th century Buddhist Sri Lanka was growing more and more powerful, and Sultan Mohammed must have been afraid of being annexed by his much larger neighbor. Converting to Islam earned him the support of the Muslim states bordering the Indian Ocean, thus keeping Sri Lanka at bay.

THOR HEYERDAHL AND THE MALDIVE MYSTERY

Thor Heyerdahl, a well-known Norwegian explorer, became fascinated with Maldives after seeing pictures of a stone statue that was uncannily similar to the figures he had previously investigated on Easter Island in the Pacific Ocean. In the mid-1980s the Maldivian government allowed him to conduct archeological research on some ancient sites, and he unearthed many artifacts that shed light on the early settlement of the islands. His discoveries lend credence to the theory that Maldives was inhabited by a well-developed Hindu and Buddhist society whose history was never documented or whose records were completely destroyed when the country adopted Islam.

One of the most important archeological finds was the buried temple complex on the island of Nilandhoo in the central atoll of Faaf. Evidence suggests there were seven temples altogether and that they were certainly Hindu because of the Hindu phallic sculptures recovered around the site. The complex is of impressive dimensions, and the temples were built of beautifully cut stones placed over a foundation of coral sand. They were shaped like pyramids. Heyerdahl also came across many limestone sculptures of Hindu gods and demons on several other islands.

On the uninhabited island of Gan in Gaaf Dhaal Atoll, Heyerdahl found evidence of Maldives' Buddhist past. In the middle of the jungle stands an impressive 3,000-year-old pyramid of enormous proportions. The explorer believes it was a stepped pyramid with ceremonial ramps on four sides, much like the ancient pyramids of Mesopotamia and pre-Columbian America. Among the artifacts recovered were the foot of a sitting Buddha, a stone bull, and two lions. The nearby island of Fuamulaku also contains several *hawitta* ("HA-wit-tah"). Called Redin's Hill by the islanders, these mounds of stone are the remnants of Buddhist bell-shaped temples. Another important site is the sunken bath made from stones of different sizes. They fit so well that it is impossible to slide a knife blade between them.

Despite all his discoveries, Heyerdahl was not able to solve the mystery of the Redin people, hence the title of the book he wrote about his investigations, *The Maldive Mystery*. He suggested that they were sun-worshipers, similar to the people of ancient Peru and Mexico. He based this theory on the fact that many mosques built on the remains of ancient temples faced the sun instead of Mecca, the holy Islamic land where Prophet Mohammed was born.

The 15 years of Portuguese occupation were the darkest in Maldivian history. Men were treated as slaves, women were violated, and a reign of terror extended to the outer atolls. The captain of the Portuguese forces, Andrea Andreas, also decreed that all Maldivians had to convert to Christianity or be put to death.

THE SULTANATE

Six dynasties ruled Maldives from 1153 to 1968, although not continuously. The Malei Dynasty produced 16 monarchs from 1153 to 1321. Two sultans and three sultanas of the Veeru Umaru Dynasty then reigned for the next 75 years. The third great dynasty was that of the Hilali. Twenty-four sultans ruled over 170 years before Maldives fell to outside forces.

The post of sultan was never hereditary; a council elected the sultan. Women were also chosen to rule as sultanas and there were always women on the ruling councils. Sultana Khadeeja Rehendhi Kabaidi Kilege, a remarkable woman, held power on three different occasions. She first became sultana in 1342 on the death of her younger brother, the previous sultan. Many scholars believe that she murdered him. In 1363 she was overthrown by her husband. But she managed to kill him and took back the throne. In 1373 her position was usurped by her second husband. The latter was also killed, and Khadeeja returned to power until her death in 1380.

PORTUGUESE OCCUPATION

At the beginning of the 16th century the Portuguese, who had already established a base in India, started to eye Maldives for its strategic location on the trade routes and its abundant supply of cowry shells. Three attempts to invade the islands were unsuccessful, but in 1558 a powerful Portuguese army under the command of Captain Andrea Andreas killed Sultan Ali VI. They were helped by the former sultan, Hassan IX, who had fled to India and converted to Christianity after a disagreement with the council of ministers. Andrea Andreas installed himself as the ruler of Maldives on behalf of Dom Emanuel, the Christian name of Hassan IX.

The Maldivians did not submit meekly to the occupation. Mohammed Thakurufaanu from the northern island of Utheemu organized a band of guerilla warriors to conduct raids against the Portuguese defenses in Male. After several years he realized that he could not oust the Portuguese on his own and sought help from the Rajah of Malabar in India. In 1573 Thakurufaanu, together with the Indian forces, launched an attack on Male and, with the help of the islanders, liberated the country from the cruel occupiers. For the next 12 years Thakurufaanu reigned as sultan and founded the Utheemu Dynasty that lasted 127 years. The day of the liberation is now celebrated as National Day each year, and Thakurufaanu is venerated as the greatest national hero of Maldivian history.

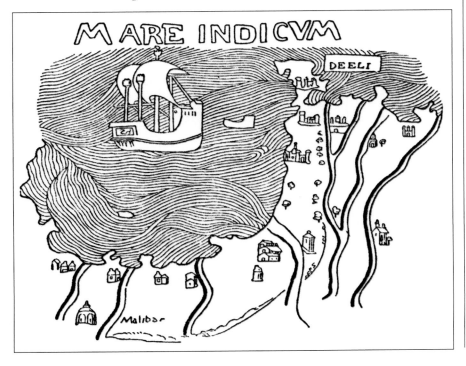

The route from the coast of Malabar to Maldives, as depicted on explorer Fra' Mauro's map.

Queen Victoria in 1882. She ruled the British Empire from 1837 to 1901.

BRITISH PROTECTORATE

Their success in helping the Maldivians fight the Portuguese gave ideas to the Malabars, who tried to invade the islands several times in the next two centuries. They finally succeeded in 1752, with the help of some Maldivians. Malabar rule, however, lasted only four months before the wily Hassan Manikufaan drove them out. This was the only other time in Maldivian history that the islands were ruled by outsiders. Manikufaan became sultan in 1759, founding the Huraage Dynasty that ruled the country until it became a republic.

Toward the end of the 18th century the British became very active in the Indian Ocean and took over Sri Lanka in 1796. As Maldives had good historical ties with Sri Lanka, relations with the British were smooth. In 1887 Sultan Mohammed Mueenuddeen II signed an agreement with Queen Victoria to turn Maldives into a British protectorate in return for an annual tribute. Two main reasons prompted this move: some Indian merchants had acquired a monopoly on foreign trade, and the sultan was afraid they would gain control over all the islands; and putting Maldives under the protection of the British crown meant that the British would not colonize the islands.

The country's first president, Amin Didi.

The protectorate worked very well for the Maldivian rulers who were left to govern the country as autocrats. The British had no power to interfere in internal matters and could only control foreign relations. What they were more interested in, especially after Sri Lanka and India became independent in 1948, was the development of a military base on the southern island of Gan.

THE REPUBLIC

In 1932 a constitution was adopted for the first time in Maldivian history that curtailed the powers of the sultan. When the elderly Sultan Abdul Majeed Didi came to power in 1943, he left the government of the country in the hands of his prime minister, Mohammed Amin Didi. The latter set about nationalizing the fish export industry and modernizing the country. Maldives was declared a republic in 1953, and Amin Didi became the country's first president. Regarded as the father of modern Maldives, he reformed the education system, revived interest in the Maldivian language and literature, and gave women a larger role in society. But his policies were too drastic, and he was overthrown a year later. Amin Didi died in 1954 after being beaten by a mob during a riot over food shortages.

Under the leadership of Gayoom, the economy of the country was liberalized, and trade increased significantly.

INDEPENDENCE

The sultanate was restored after Amin Didi's death and lasted until 1968. The British started developing their air base on Gan in 1956, bringing work and much prosperity to the southern atolls. When Ibrahim Nasir became prime minister in 1957, he called for a review of the agreement to lease Gan to the British. This angered the inhabitants of Addu and Huvadhoo atolls. In 1959, claiming that they were ill-treated by the central government, the two atolls declared independence as the United Suvadive Islands. Three years later Nasir sent gunboats to the southern atolls, and the elected president of the Suvadive Islands was forced to flee to the Seychelles.

On July 26, 1965, the British lifted the protectorate, and Maldives became an independent sovereign nation. British forces, however, remained on Gan until 1976. Following a referendum in 1968, the sultanate was definitively abolished, and a new republic was established. Nasir was elected president, and he ruled for 10 years, serving two terms. By 1978, dissatisfaction over the spiraling prices of food led the population to protest against the president. Fearing for his life, Nasir resigned and fled to Singapore.

Maumoon Abdul Gayoom was elected president to replace Nasir. Adopting a more consultative and open style of government, he was immensely popular and survived three coup attempts—in 1980, 1983, and 1988. Under his leadership, Maldives opened up to tourism and experienced good economic growth. Because people enjoyed prosperity under his rule, Gayoom was reelected five times.

A MAN FOR ALL ISLANDS

Born in Male in 1937, Maumoon Abdul Gayoom's intelligence was apparent when he received a scholarship at the age of 10, the youngest person to be sent overseas by the government. He went on to study in Sri Lanka and Egypt, where he obtained a master's degree in Islamic Studies. He also studied law and philosophy.

Before being elected president in 1978, Gayoom worked in various government departments and was Maldives' first permanent representative to the United Nations. He was a lecturer in Islamic law and philosophy in Nigeria from 1969 to 1971. In a policy statement in 1979 he committed himself to give greater freedom to the people and to follow democratic procedures. Gayoom was himself a victim of repression during the Nasir years when he was banished from Male in 1973. During his 20 years in power, he brought political and economic stability to the islands through constitutional changes and sound economic policies. Despite his overwhelming popularity in Maldives, he is accused by some human rights organizations of leading a repressive Muslim system that does not tolerate dissent. On the other hand Muslim fundamentalists insist that he is not doing enough to turn the country into a truly Islamic state.

One of the achievements of Maumoon Abdul Gayoom in the international arena has been to highlight the plight of small island states in the face of increased industrialization. He was one of the first world leaders to caution against global warming. Taking part in forums and international conferences, he tirelessly repeats his message that the industrialized world is accountable to small island states for the rise in sea levels, and that countries such as Maldives are in danger of disappearing. As he states in his biography, he is "a man for all islands."

GOVERNMENT

MALDIVES IS A DEMOCRATIC REPUBLIC that is inspired by Islam. The present constitution, adopted in 1968, has been amended several times in 1970, 1972, and 1975. It provides for the basic rights of the people, such as freedom of speech and assembly, equality before the law, and the right to own property. Nevertheless the various governments have not always upheld these rights, in particular freedom of speech and assembly. The government is empowered to punish all opposition, and many actions and words considered fair criticism in Western countries would fall under the category of treason or subversion in Maldives.

The people of Maldives are called Maldivian citizens. Anyone above the age of 21 has the right to vote in presidential as well as legislative elections. Younger Maldivians, especially those who have studied overseas, are becoming increasingly vocal in their demands for more freedom.

Left: **The national pledge of Maldives.**

Opposite: **President Gayoom meeting citizens of Male before the recent presidential election.**

President Maumoon Abdul Gayoom has been elected president six times.

THE LEGISLATIVE STRUCTURE

The government of Maldives is composed of a unicameral assembly called the Citizens' *Majlis* ("MADGE-liss"). Made up of 48 representatives, the Majlis enacts laws and approves the annual budget. The 19 administrative atolls and the island of Male elect two representatives each, and eight others are appointed by the president. There are no political parties in Maldives, and representatives are elected based on personal achievements.

The Special Majlis is a separate body that gathers on a temporary basis to make amendments to the constitution. It is made up of cabinet ministers, the 48 members of the Citizens' Majlis, and 48 other individuals, mainly religious leaders and atoll elders.

Nominated by the Majlis, the presidential candidate goes through a national referendum to determine whether the population agrees with the Majlis' choice. Presidential elections are held every five years and do not coincide with legislative elections. The president holds enormous power in Maldives. He appoints the cabinet of ministers in charge of

NATIONAL SYMBOLS

The Maldivian flag consists of a green rectangle surrounded by a red border. In the center is a white crescent with the tips facing away from the flag post. The red border symbolizes the blood of the Maldivians who fought for the freedom of their country. The green rectangle represents life, progress, and prosperity. The white crescent in the center of the flag denotes the Islamic faith of the nation.

The national emblem consists of a coconut palm rising from a crescent and a star, and flanked by two national flags. Underneath is a scroll with the traditional title of the country written in Arabic. The coconut represents the livelihood of the country because of its many uses in daily life. The crescent and star represent Islam, while the two flags are symbols of authority. The words *Ad-Dawlat Al-Mahaldheebiyya* written on the scroll mean "The State of Maldives" in Arabic. The emblem is usually reproduced on a light blue background to represent the importance of the ocean to Maldives.

governing the country as well as the judges. The judiciary is not independent of the executive council. The constitution also makes the president the guardian of Islam in the country. Like in many other countries, the Maldivian president is also in charge of national defense. At present the cabinet is composed of 16 ministers. These ministers need not be elected members of the Majlis. The president simply selects the best people for the job.

THE JUDICIARY

The legal system in Maldives is based on the Islamic Sharia law combined with some English common law, in particular in the area of commercial law. The head of the judiciary is the chief justice, who is usually a highly respected Islamic scholar. The chief justice, together with two other judges, presides over the High Court, which also serves as the court of appeal. All three are appointed by the president. Every inhabited island has its own court of law. Male has eight courts.

THE PRESIDENT'S CONSULTATIVE COUNCIL

The President's Consultative Council was set up in 1985 by President Gayoom in an attempt to involve more capable young people in the process of decision-making. This think tank consists of 55 members who are selected from outside the government. Cabinet ministers, assembly members, as well as members of the presidential secretariat are all ineligible. The Consultative Council offers an avenue for young people to reach the president and to voice their hopes and aspirations.

ATOLL ADMINISTRATION

The archipelago is divided into 20 administrative units, composed of the island of Male and 19 atolls. Although they are called atolls, they do not coincide with the geographical atolls. Some administrative atolls are actually made up of more than one atoll, while others are only half an atoll. The 19 atolls are: Alif, Baa, Dhaal, Faaf, Gaaf Alif, Gaaf Dhaal, Gnaviyani, Haa Alif, Haa Dhaal, Kaafu, Laamu, Lhaviyani, Meemu, Noonu, Raa, Seenu, Shaviyani, Thaa, and Vaavu.

Each atoll is governed by an atoll chief called *atolhu varin* ("AH-toh-loo VAH-rin"). This person functions as the governor of a province. He receives legal advice from the *ghaazee* ("HAR-zee"), the religious head of the atoll. The atoll chief is appointed by the president and tends to come from an influential family residing in the capital of the atoll. He is responsible for the economic and political direction of the atoll.

Every inhabited island is supervised by a *katheeb* ("KAH-teeb"), who is an official appointed by the government. The island chief, usually a distinguished island citizen, has a number of full-time officials, called *kuda katheeb* ("KOO-da KAH-teeb"), to help him run the island. They in turn work together with an island council. The island chief is an important personage; any islander summoned by the *katheeb*'s office would go immediately. Justice is delivered by the local magistrate, but serious cases are referred to the courts in Male.

NATIONAL DEFENSE

The National Security Service (NSS) is responsible for the defense of the country. Besides military duties, it also performs police and maritime duties. Its mission is to preserve internal security and patrol the country's territorial waters for smugglers and illegal fishermen. Made up of about 2,000 personnel, the NSS also guards the airport, and the president and other important officials. The NSS is stationed in Male.

Although there is no universal draft in Maldives, some young men who have completed 10th grade may be called on to join the NSS for two years. About 10% are selected at random every year. This service is a way of paying back the government for having given them an education. However, if a young man has more talent in another field, he may perform his national service in another department.

CRIME AND PUNISHMENT

Maldives follows a moderate version of the Muslim Sharia law that does not use extreme physical punishment. Although the crime rate is very low, many actions are classified as being criminal in nature. Most of the crimes investigated in Maldives concern inappropriate sexual relations and the consumption of alcohol. Petty

MALDIVES AND THE WORLD

Maldives has diplomatic relations with over 50 countries and is a member of numerous international organizations, including the United Nations and the British Commonwealth. Through President Gayoom, the country has been very active in the nonaligned movement and strongly supports the demilitarization of the Indian Ocean. An instance of the Maldivian government's strong desire for peace was its refusal to rent the former British air base on Gan to the Soviet Union for $1 million in 1977. For one of the least developed countries in the world, it was a strong demonstration of political willpower. As an Islamic state, Maldives is also very close to Arab nations and is a member of the Organization of the Islamic Conference.

It is in the South Asian Association for Regional Cooperation (SAARC) and the Alliance of Small Island States (AOSIS) that Maldives has made its mark. Set up in 1985, the seven-member SAARC aims to boost trade among member countries and to offer a unified front in the face of foreign intervention. Maldives chaired the leaders' summit twice, in 1990 and 1997. Among the proposals put forward by the country were the need to pay more attention to the children of SAARC countries and the designation of 1992 as the "SAARC Year of the Environment." Maldives also did much to defuse tensions between member countries India and Pakistan whenever relations between the two neighbors hit a low.

Being at the forefront of the battle against global warming, Maldives was instrumental in setting up AOSIS in 1992. It was after a conference in Male on the rise in sea levels that the organization came into being. A grouping of 42 small island states in Asia, the Pacific, the Atlantic Ocean, and the Caribbean seas, the alliance concentrates on climatic change and other environmental issues. Maldives speaks on behalf of small island states in the international arena.

theft and white-collar crimes are on the rise. Crimes in the islands are investigated by the island chief since there are no police stationed in the atolls. Victims of crime have to personally accuse a suspect in court. To secure a conviction for alcohol consumption, two witnesses have to be present, while adultery requires four eyewitnesses.

The punishment of choice in Maldives is banishment to a remote island for periods ranging from eight months to 12 years. Political dissidents are kept in high-security jails in outlying islands. Banishment can be psychologically very damaging because the person is cut off completely from family and friends and his or her familiar environment. Families of banished persons often arrange for them to be looked after by a local family, and when the period of banishment is over, they are eventually welcomed back into their island community. Some prisoners even keep in touch with their host communities after they have returned home.

Opposite: **A member of the National Security Service patrolling at a street parade.**

ECONOMY

FROM ONE OF THE 20 POOREST COUNTRIES in the world 20 years ago, Maldives is now about halfway down the list of 180 countries surveyed by the United Nations. In the year 2000 the country was taken off the list of least developed countries by the UN Development Program. For a country with almost no natural resources, this is quite an achievement.

Maldives has been able to record an annual economic growth of around 9% in the past 20 years due to sound policies and financial aid from the United Nations, the World Bank, and developed countries such as Japan and the oil-rich Arab states. Traditionally Maldivians made a living from fishing and subsistence agriculture; today it is tourism that brings in more revenue. Maldives has also embarked on a light industrialization program.

Left and opposite: **Tourism contributes a substantial amount of foreign currency to the country.**

FISHING

Each fisherman can catch up to 100 fish in an hour. On good days, the boat's hold fills up in a couple of hours. Maldivian fishermen always go back to their islands before sunset.

Until the early 1970s the major economic activity was fishing. It is still the second source of foreign exchange and employs 22% of the labor force. Maldives claims a 200-mile (322-km) exclusive economic zone, so the country has an enormous supply of fish. Every man in Maldives has engaged in fishing at one time or another, even if it is just to catch the day's meal. Those who are in between jobs know that they can always fall back on fishing to make a living.

Fishing in Maldives is still carried on in the traditional manner, using rod or lines and hooks. Nets are never used for they are ecologically very damaging to marine life. For this reason Maldivian fish exports are certified dolphin-safe. The catch is mostly skipjack tuna, but yellowfin tuna, little tuna, mackerel, and sharks are also caught. Islanders go out to sea in the early morning, immediately after dawn prayers. A crew of eight or nine takes its place in the boat, and they do not have to go very far to get their catch.

FISH PROCESSING

Most of the fish is processed before being exported to Europe and Asia. The best fish are chilled and flown immediately to Japan to be made into sashimi. The rest are frozen, canned, salted, or smoked. Fish for freezing and canning are taken to the processing plant on Felivaru in Lhaviyani Atoll. Salting and smoking are carried out on a few uninhabited islands. The fish are gutted at night, when the sun is down. They are then placed into containers of salt to be preserved. After they have absorbed the salt, they are laid out to dry in the sun. "Maldive fish," which is very popular in the islands and in Sri Lanka, is a unique product of Maldives. After the fish has been gutted and filleted, it is boiled in salted water. The boiled fish is then smoked above a wood fire. To preserve it further, it is left to dry in the sun. "Maldive fish" keeps for a very long period.

Fishermen's Day on December 10 highlights the importance of fishing in the country. This festival celebrates the contribution of fishermen to the economy.

TOURISM

"Maldives must develop quality tourism, always giving tourists what they want. They used to come here with sandwiches, now they can eat gourmet standard meals in fine dining restaurants set in lush, tropical gardens." Resort owner Mohammed Umar Maniku.

A recent addition to the economy, tourism started in earnest in 1972 with the opening of the first resort on Kurumba Island. The Maldivian government was quick to tap into this new source of income and drew up a master plan to see the industry into the 21st century. Tourists come to Maldives to dive among the impressive marine life and relax on the beautiful beaches. Most of them are Europeans, but Asians are coming in greater numbers. Tourism is the top foreign exchange earner and the fastest growing sector of the economy.

Maldivian tourism policy aims to offer guests quality accommodation and services in order to generate maximum revenue. To protect the local population's Muslim culture, tourists are isolated in their resorts. They also do not have much contact with local people. This sense of isolation is actually one of the reasons nearly 300,000 tourists are drawn to Maldives every year.

Tourist resorts are built only on uninhabited islands, and tourists need a permit to visit the inhabited islands other than Male if they are on their own and not part of an organized group. More than 70 islands have been earmarked for resort development. The older resorts are located in Male Atoll, but as demand rises, other islands in the central atolls have been given over to tourism.

Resort operators lease the island from the government and have to follow the strict Tourism Law concerning environmental standards. For example they need a permit to cut down trees during the construction of the hotel and are not allowed to import water from any of the inhabited islands. Maldives Association of Tourism Industry is a private sector organization of resort owners, tour agencies, and diving schools. It maps out policies and helps to promote tourism in the country.

AGRICULTURE

Maldivian soil is very poor, and only about 10% of the total land area is suitable for agriculture. To meet the growing demands of the population, large quantities of fresh vegetables, fruit, and meat must be imported, especially for the tourist industry. The government actively encourages the agricultural sector to prevent a drain of much-needed foreign reserves.

Large-scale agriculture is carried out on more than 800 uninhabited islands leased from the government. As the islands have no natural source of water, such as rivers or lakes, the growing of crops depends on natural rainfall during the southwest monsoon. Maldivian planters use mainly organic fertilizers and rotate their crops for a better yield.

Despite the limitations, the agricultural sector still manages to produce a number of cash crops. The most bountiful is the coconut, and its production remains the dominant agricultural activity. Coconuts are eaten and can be used to make a variety of products from soap to rope. Other food crops include breadfruit, root vegetables, and fruit. Islanders in the southern atolls continue to cultivate and consume taro, cassava, and sweet potatoes. The cultivation of millet and maize has almost disappeared, as Maldivians today rely more heavily on rice as a staple food.

Many women tend a vegetable garden to grow some food for the family. They also keep some chickens for meat and eggs, as well as a goat for milk.

A farmer harvesting watermelons. Papayas, limes, bananas, and watermelons have a higher commercial value as they are in great demand in the resorts. The island of Thoddoo produces the best watermelons in the country.

Although some measure of mechanization has been implemented, most industries are still very labor-intensive.

INDUSTRY

The industrial sector includes traditional occupations and modern industry. Traditional occupations, such as boat building, weaving, rope making, and handicraft-making, have received a new lease on life with the advent of tourism. This sector employs about a quarter of the labor force, mainly women, since the products are made by hand. Modern industry includes fish canning, garment manufacturing, and the making of PVC pipes.

The industrial sector accounts for about 6% of the gross domestic product (GDP). The Maldivian government is aware that this sector must grow in order to meet the demands of the economy. However, the small size of the domestic market, lack of infrastructure, shortage of skilled workers, and lack of raw materials pose serious problems to the development of this sector.

TRADE

Maldives imports much more than it exports. All imports in 1996 totaled $302 million and consisted mainly of petroleum products, machinery, and consumer goods, including food. In the same year the country exported $59 million worth of goods. Marine exports accounted for most of all exports, the major items being frozen and dried skipjack tuna. Other exports included clothing and scrap metal.

Singapore supplies Maldives with almost a third of all imported goods. Not all the products originate in Singapore, which is a very convenient consignment place and where suppliers offer favorable credit. Sri Lanka is another important trading partner, both providing imports and absorbing exports. More than one-fifth of all exports goes to the United Kingdom, with which Maldives has retained excellent relations. The United States, Germany, and Japan also buy Maldivian goods.

THE MALDIVIAN CURRENCY

The rufiyaa (Rf) is the unit of money used in Maldives. It is divided into 100 laari. Bank notes come in denominations of 2, 5, 10, 20, 50, 100, and 500 rufiyaa. Very pretty and colorful, they feature objects that are typically Maldivian, such as coconuts or fishing boats. Coins in circulation are 2, 5, 10, 25, and 50 laari, and 1 and 2 rufiyaa. The first three have dimpled edges. The rufiyaa became the national currency in 1948. Coins were first minted in the late 16th century, but they were shaped like hairpins and not round.

With easy access to the sea, Maldives was a veritable mint when cowry shells were used as the unit of currency by the countries in the Indian Ocean. The islanders devised a way of collecting them by placing palm fronds in the shallow waters. When the fronds were laden with cowries, they were pulled onto the beach where the cowries were left to die in the sun. The shells were then buried in the sand so that the animals decomposed underground, leaving only the shiny shells.

Tourists fly to their resorts by seaplane *(above)* or helicopter. Both boats and planes are owned by private operators, and there are no scheduled regular services.

TRANSPORT AND COMMUNICATION

Most islands are so small that the inhabitants go everywhere on foot or by bicycle. Nevertheless cars, including taxis, do exist, especially on Male, where there is a vehicle for every 17.5 yards (16 m) of road. To travel from one island to another, Maldivians use speedboats or ferries. The national airline, Air Maldives, flies to the Middle East, India, Sri Lanka, and Malaysia, and also operates domestic flights to the five airports in the islands. Most tourists arrive by charter flights.

The people of Male and the resort islands have easy access to telephones, fax service, and the Internet. Phone ownership is high on Male. The telecommunications network is now being extended to the rest of the archipelago and all inhabited islands will receive telecommunications facilities by the end of the year 2000.

DHONI

The traditional boat of Maldives is the caravel-styled *dhoni* ("DOE-nih"). Almost every family in the islands owns a small *dhoni*. With its distinctive tall, curved prow, it is strong and built to last. Equipped with a diesel engine, the long and slender boat has a fabric roof, a wooden bench running down each side, and a sail as a backup. The helmsman uses his legs to steer the vessel. He sits or stands on the flat stern, holding the tiller with his foot and trolling a fishing line. *Dhoni* come in all sizes and are used for fishing as well as for transport. An *odi* ("O-dih") is a large *dhoni* used for cargo.

The basic design of the *dhoni* has hardly changed over the centuries. The best *dhoni* are built in Raa Atoll by master craftsmen who pass on their skill from generation to generation. These builders command a lot of respect as well as high salaries. They do not need to draw building plans, and the construction can take a few months because the carpenter uses only his hands and a few tools. *Dhoni* are traditionally made of coconut wood in a thatched hut at the water's edge. The hull is constructed from planks of hardwood taken from the base of the tree and fitted together with wooden nails like a precise jigsaw puzzle. The whole boat is secured with copper nails and wooden pegs. Once completed, the *dhoni* is painted all over with fish oil to preserve the wood and ease its launch into the water.

MALDIVIANS

AN OFFICIAL ESTIMATE IN JULY 1999 put the population of Maldives at 300,220. Although this figure seems low in absolute terms, Maldives is classified as the seventh most densely populated country in the world. With improvements in health services, the population is rapidly increasing. Life expectancy is 66 years for men and 70 years for women. Nearly 80% of the population is below the age of 35. Women form about 49% of the population.

About a quarter of the Maldivians live in Male, which is experiencing such severe overcrowding that it has embarked on a land reclamation program. In the other inhabited islands, the population is spread out quite unevenly. The larger islands, especially those that have easy access to good fishing, are more popular, with as many as 3,000 persons on one island. In general each island is home to between 200 and 800 people.

Left and opposite: **Most Maldivian children live with their parents and their mother's extended family within the same compound.**

A MELTING POT

Maldivians say that the earliest inhabitants of their country were the Redins, the builders of the archeological ruins found on some of the islands. Tall and big, the Redins had brown hair and light skin. Their faces were long and they had blue eyes. Norwegian ethnologist and author Thor Heyerdahl speculated that they worshiped the sun, in the same way that pre-Columbian people in South America did. The mystery of the Redins will probably never be solved since none of today's Maldivians can trace their ancestry back to them.

The people of Maldives present a melting pot of ethnic influences. Most of them are dark-skinned and have straight black hair and black eyes. They are attractive and not very tall. In physical appearance, they are closer to the Indians and Sri Lankans. The fairer ones may be descended from the Portuguese who occupied the islands in the 16th century. The Maldivians also have traces of Arab and African blood. Maldivians swear that they can tell which island people come from by the way they walk.

ETHNIC COMMUNITIES

The Giraaveru people claim to be the aboriginal inhabitants of Maldives. Descended from the

Tamils of south India, they are indistinguishable from the rest of the population in physical appearance. However, they have always kept to themselves and maintained a separate identity. The Giraaveru follow different customs and speak with a different accent. The women tie their hair in a bun on the right side of the head instead of the usual practice of tying it on the left side. After their island was badly affected by soil erosion, the Giraaveru were moved to the island of Hulule in 1968. They later resettled in the western quarter of Male when the airport was expanded.

The descendants of Indian traders who came to Maldives in the 19th century make up a distinct ethnic and religious minority. A few hundred in numbers, they are also Muslims. A number of Sri Lankans have also settled in Maldives, mainly to work in the bars in resort hotels because the Muslim locals do not touch alcohol.

The survival of the Giraaveru as a distinct community is in danger because many young people marry other Maldivians and get absorbed into the mainstream society. There are fewer than 150 Giraaveru today.

THE NATIONAL CHARACTER

One of the striking aspects of the Maldivian character is the lack of obvious emotion. They are a quiet people who are not given to expressive demonstrations. Children are taught to keep their thoughts and feelings to themselves, even within the family. Thus they do not appear to be close to each other, especially to their fathers. When Maldivians meet their friends, they do not seem to be particularly happy. The Maldivian language has no words for "hello" and "thank you," and there are very few expressions of concern. Maldivians take time to warm up to strangers, although they show utmost courtesy at all times.

There is a large element of stoic resignation in the Maldivian approach to life. Surrounded by the sea and sometimes living at the mercy of the elements, they take nothing for granted. Maldivians are a peaceful people who do not relish confrontation.

Opposite: **A fisherman mending his fishing net.**

Southerners in their homes.

THE SOUTHERN MINORITY

Physically separated from the rest of Maldives by the deep One-and-a-Half-Degree Channel, the people of the southernmost atolls have long felt distinct from Male. They speak their own dialect, which is more related to early Sinhalese, the language of Sri Lanka, than to Dhivehi, the language of Maldives. Most Maldivians do not understand the southern dialect. The southerners also once had direct trade links with Sri Lanka.

Underlying tensions between the south and Male came to a peak in the 1950s and 1960s when the government stopped the southerners from selling their "Maldive fish" directly to Sri Lankan traders. Islanders were also forbidden from being employed by the British military base that had just been set up on Gan. In 1959, under the leadership of Abdulla Afif Didi, the three southern atolls joined the United Suvadive Islands and broke away from Male. They formed a People's Council, elected Didi as president, and established a trading corporation and a bank. The rebellion was short-lived, for the Maldivian government sent armed troops in 1962 to bring the southerners to heel. The soldiers destroyed all the homes on Thinadhoo, the capital of Huvadhoo Atoll, forcing the people to flee to neighboring islands. They did not return until four years later. Didi fled to the Seychelles, but he is still talked about on his home island of Hithadhoo.

Today the Maldivian government encourages the development of the southern atolls. Foreign investors have set up industries in the islands, especially on Gan.

WOMEN

Women in Maldives have equal rights under the law. They can run for office, manage a business, and own land and houses. Although women cannot be judges or priests, they have access to equal educational and employment opportunities. The Ministry of Women's Affairs, run by the only female minister, looks after the development of women.

Women lead an active economic and social life. In the evening, island women like to meet on their verandahs and have a good chat. In Male, groups of women like to go for a stroll in the evening.

Married women enjoy a certain amount of independence. They can retain their maiden name and exercise much control over family matters. They can acquire land or property. About one-third of the houses and coconut trees in the islands belong to women. In most villages women are the heads of the household because the men go to work in the resorts or are out fishing all day. An inheritance is split among all the children, regardless of gender.

Maldivian women are quite conservative in their dress and behavior, but they are not required to cover themselves from head to toe as in some Muslim countries. In fact, the law does not allow them to conceal their faces.

FAMILY LIFE

The family forms the basis of Maldivian society. About 80% of Maldivian households are nuclear families composed of a married couple and their children rather than an extended family. The extended family, however, lives within the same compound and helps to look after the children. It is usually the mother's family that is assigned this task. Maldivian families tend to be very large, with as many as eight to 10 children. A program for birth control has been set up, but it is only available to married couples and not many islanders believe in it. Children live with their parents until they get married and set up their own household.

Families wake up very early to say their morning prayers, between 4:30 and 5:00 A.M. Fishermen get ready for the day and set off before sunrise. Women prepare breakfast, clean the house, and get the children ready for school. All outdoor work is carried out by the men while women are in charge of all household chores.

The family meets twice a day for meals. When they are together, they say very little to each other and rarely express any emotion. People talk very softly, even to the children. Few children speak to their fathers.

SOCIAL STRUCTURE

Maldives practiced the caste system well into the 1920s. Although the castes have been abolished, Maldivians still put a lot of emphasis on social classes and wealth. Traditionally there was a significant gap between the elite in Male and the population of the other islands. This gap is slowly closing with the government's policy of raising the standard of living in the outer islands. Nevertheless the influential families in Male, such as the Kaloa, Fulu, Maniku, and Didi, who used to be very close to the sultan, still control the government and business sectors. They also furnish the country's religious leaders, professionals, and scholars.

In the islands the atoll chief, island chief, and religious magistrate are the most important people. The boat owner is also at the top of the social structure. He employs all the fishermen. Next on the social ladder are the boat builders and the medicine men. Skilled craftsmen also command a lot of respect. At the bottom of the ladder is the toddy tapper. He looks after the coconuts and taps their sap to make syrup and the toddy drink.

Above: **A large Maldivian family.**

Opposite: **Girls collect water from the well and carry it home in metal pots perched on their heads.**

LIFESTYLE

DESPITE THE DEVELOPMENT OF TOURISM, not much has changed in the Maldivian style of life. Daily activities revolve around Islam and religious observances. The government has certainly brought vast improvements to the life of islanders, but their lifestyle is still very much defined by the sea. Fishing and fish-related activities are their main concerns.

Male, however, has experienced enormous changes in the past 20 years. Land reclaimation has enlarged the island, tall buildings are replacing the one-story coral houses, and modern telecommunications have brought the rest of the world to Maldives. Thus young people from the islands look at Male as the epitome of modernity. They come here for education or to find work. To the islander, it is in Male that one can acquire great wealth and enjoy the comforts of modern life.

Young people in Male *(left)* **are well informed, follow the latest fashions, and wish for a more Westernized lifestyle, while their counterparts living in rural areas** *(opposite)* **are content with their peaceful lives. Male children yearn to go overseas and experience firsthand what they have read about or seen on television.**

MARRIAGE AND DIVORCE

Maldivians marry early, the legal age being 15 for women. Most newly married couples are in the 20–24 age group. They also marry often. There is no stigma attached to a woman who has been married before, and it is not uncommon for some men to have had 20 wives.

Although some modern couples in Male choose to get married in Western dress and throw a party for their guests, most people keep their wedding simple. The ceremony, celebrated by the local judge or *ghaazee*, takes place in the groom's house or the island office. Present are the groom, his father, the bride's uncle, and two witnesses. Prior to the ceremony, the groom has received the consent of the bride and her father. The man must pay his wife a "bride price," but the woman does not have to bring a dowry. After marriage, the couple usually lives with the wife's parents.

According to Islam, a man may have up to four wives at a time if he can afford it and if he treats them all equally, but a woman cannot be married to more than one man at a time. Most Maldivian men, however, cannot afford to keep more than one wife. The wealthier fishermen or traveling boatmen may have wives on several islands. Most people get married because sex outside marriage is illegal and adultery is a serious crime.

Divorce is as easy as marriage. A man can divorce his wife simply by telling her that he is divorcing her and then reporting it to the local judge. But women have to ask their husbands' permission to divorce or take their case to the judge and prove that they have been ill-treated. In theory, it is possible for a couple to be married one day and divorced the next. For three months after the divorce, a woman cannot remarry except to the ex-husband. This is to allow for reconciliation and to make sure that she is not pregnant. A man, however, can marry immediately after divorce. At 59%, Maldives has one of the highest divorce rates in the world.

Although it is traditional for Maldivians to marry and divorce often, the government is urging the population not to be too hasty in dissolving their marriages. To prevent the disintegration of families and family values, President Gayoom himself stresses that divorce should be used as a last resort.

VILLAGE LIFE

Villages are laid out on a rectangular plan, with each family leasing an area of 49 feet (15 m) by 98 feet (30 m) from the government. The main house is in the center of the compound and is used for sleeping. The kitchen and bathroom are separate structures within the compound. Maldivian bathrooms do not have roofs. By tradition, someone climbing a coconut tree near a house is supposed to shout to announce his presence to those using the open-air bathroom. Houses are made of coral or thatched palm fronds. Families spend much of their time in the shade of trees in the garden or on the verandah.

Maldivian men chatting in the village square.

The village square is a platform of logs located on the beach or in a central location near the sea. It is constructed in the shade of a large tree. The men of the village come to the square to relax, play cards or chess, or sleep. As everybody comes to the square at some time or other, important notices are posted on the trunk of the tree.

Apart from a field where young men and boys play soccer, there are no other amenities for children. They play in the sea or on the beach. Adults, however, have a social club that looks after their welfare.

Villages are quiet and peaceful. They are virtually devoid of any male presence during the day because the men are out fishing. Women and girls keep the sandy streets clean by sweeping them with a broom made from the spines of coconut leaves. Each woman is in charge of the public ground in front of her compound. A few times a week, the village women get together to sweep the beach and other public areas.

EDUCATION

Although education is not compulsory, most children do go to school. The government has placed much emphasis on education in the last 20 years, and most parents see the benefits of sending their children to school. The Maldivian education system is based on the British system, although instruction is in Dhivehi ("DEE-vay-hih"), the local language, in the first few years. Today Maldives has a literacy rate of 93.2%, making it the most literate country in South Asia and the Indian Ocean region.

Children start their education at the age of 3 in religious schools called *makthab* ("MOK-tub"). In the islands this may be under the shade of a tree

Most schools are single sex and children wear uniforms in school. Even when a school is co-educational, the boys are seated separate from the girls.

on the beach or in a small room. Young children receive religious instruction and learn to read and write in Dhivehi and Arabic. At the age of 6, they enroll in a primary school. Every atoll has at least one government primary school. Standards are high, and students are expected to read and write in Dhivehi, English, and Arabic by the age of 7. Secondary school starts in the sixth grade when the children are 10 years old and ends with 10th grade. Children learn Dhivehi, English, mathematics, science, fine arts, environmental studies, and calligraphy. Those who wish to continue their studies must transfer to a school in Male for 11th and 12th grades and take the British GCE "A" level examination. There is no higher education facility in Maldives and young people who want to attend university must go overseas. English is introduced as a second language in the first grade and is the medium of instruction in grades 9 and 10.

A local school in Maldives.

Above: **Young nurses at a local hospital.**

Opposite: **A Maldivian man in a sarong.**

HEALTHCARE

Maldives has made such spectacular progress in healthcare that life expectancy has jumped by 20 years since 1980. Communicable diseases have also been kept under control, with no cases of malaria reported in the past 10 years. The infant mortality rate has also declined together with the birth rate.

The main hospital in Maldives is the Indira Gandhi Memorial Hospital in Male. The 200-bed facility provides a wide range of medical services with 15 areas of specialization. There is also a smaller private hospital in Male with facilities for surgery. There are another five regional hospitals located in the central, north, and south atolls.

Basic healthcare is provided by the family health workers stationed on every inhabited island. Their job is to provide vaccination to children and pregnant women, promote family planning, and control communicable diseases such as malaria and tuberculosis. One vital aspect of their mission is to educate the island population about healthy practices and the importance of hygiene in their daily activities. For more serious medical treatment, islanders go to the atoll health center where there is at least one doctor.

Many Maldivians also consult a local medicine man or woman whom they call the *hakeem* ("HAH-keem"). These traditional practitioners believe that good health depends on the balance between the hot, cold, dry, and wet properties of the body. Thus, when someone has a fever, they recommend "cold" foods and herbal remedies. For the flu the patient has to eat dry fish. The *hakeem* is treated with great respect in the island communities.

MALE DRESS

As befitting an Islamic nation, Maldivians dress very conservatively. Although the tropical climate means that the weather is very hot, the Maldivian islanders do not like to expose their skin. Most men in Male wear trousers and a short-sleeved shirt. Office workers usually wear long sleeves with a tie. Fishermen and other

village folks, given the nature of their work, prefer a casual and comfortable attire. They usually wear a T-shirt above a sarong, which is a piece of cloth that is tied around the waist and reaches to the ankles. When they go into the sea, they hitch up the sarong to turn it into a loincloth.

FEMALE DRESS

Women in Male can be seen wearing Western dresses and even short skirts. The usual attire, however, is a brightly-colored long sleeved dress that reaches just below the knees. Like the village men, they also wear the sarong, but it is worn underneath the dress, like a petticoat. More fashionable women like to go out in a discreetly patterned dress that reaches the ankles and has long sleeves. It has a high waist and a distinctive wide collar embroidered with gold and silver thread. The embroidery takes weeks to complete. The dress is worn tight across the arms and chest and loose over the hips. Women complete the outfit with a headscarf that is pinned to the hair without covering it completely. The village women wear more conservative and casual clothes because their work requires them to be comfortably dressed.

WORKING HOURS

Maldivians start work early and end early. The working week is from Sunday to Thursday. Government officers start their day at 7:30 a.m. and finish at 1:30 p.m. Many government workers have a second job in the afternoon to earn extra cash to make ends meet. Some senior officers operate resorts when they are off duty. The private sector starts later, between 8:30 and 9, but basically has the same number of working hours. Shops open between 6 and 8 and close between 9 and 11. All offices, shops, and eating places close for 15 minutes four times a day for prayers. Working hours are shortened during the Ramadan, the Muslim fasting month.

Above: **Workers getting a lift to their workplace.**

Opposite: **Women in modern dress.**

RELIGION

THE EARLIEST INHABITANTS OF MALDIVES were probably worshipers of the sun. Ruins that have been unearthed show places of worship facing the setting sun in the west. Today's Maldivians still retain some of these beliefs in their superstitions. When settlers from India moved south to the islands, they brought with them their Hindu religion. Hinduism was later supplanted by Buddhism brought by the Sri Lankans. However, with the arrival of Islam in the 12th century, both Hinduism and Buddhism disappeared completely. Maldivian children are taught the story of the conversion to show them how powerful their religion is. Today Islam is the only religion allowed in the country, and the country is 100% Sunni Muslim. As the president is the guardian of the faith, according to the constitution, Islam pervades every aspect of life, and there is little distinction between the religious and the secular.

Left: **Muslims praying quietly in a mosque.**

Opposite: **A girl learns to read the Holy Koran.**

A poster of the Islamic city of Mecca.

THE ISLAMIC FAITH

Started in the 7th century by Prophet Mohammed, Islam is the religion of most of the Arab world. It shares many common characteristics with Judaism and Christianity, the other two religions present in the region at that time. Called Muslims, followers of Islam believe in one single God (Allah) who is all-powerful. They also believe in all the Jewish and Christian prophets, but think that it was Mohammed who received the word of Allah. Muslims do not ascribe any godlike qualities to Mohammed but revere him as the mouthpiece of Allah. Saying or doing anything against Islam is a serious crime in Maldives, and foreigners have been sentenced to jail or banishment for trying to promote other religions.

Born in Mecca in A.D. 570, Mohammed started having visions in the year 610. Claiming to act on the instructions of Allah, he launched a campaign against idolatry and injustice. The people of Mecca did not have any

THE FIVE PILLARS OF ISLAM

1. *Shahadah* ("sha-HAH-dah") is the declaration of the Islamic faith that "There is no God but Allah, and Mohammed is his prophet."
2. *Salat* ("sah-LAT") or *namadh* ("na-MAHD") is the call to prayer. All Muslims must pray five times a day facing Mecca. (As some of the mosques in Maldives are built atop older structures that face the raising sun, the faithful sometimes have to say their prayers in a rather awkward position, for example, facing a corner, such as in the Friday Mosque in Male.)
3. *Zakat* ("za-KAHT") is the act of giving charity to the needy.
4. *Ramadan* ("RA-mah-dan") is the ninth month of the Islamic calendar. During this period, all Muslims must fast during the day.
5. *Haj* ("HAJJ") is the pilgrimage to Mecca that should be done at least once in the lifetime of every Muslim.

religion at that time. Mohammed soon gained a large following, especially among the poor and downtrodden, and was persecuted by those in power. He managed to defeat his persecutors and imposed Islam throughout most of Arabia. With enormous zeal, his followers spread the religion beyond the Middle East after his death.

RELIGIOUS PRACTICES

The teachings of Allah are set down in the Koran ("KOH-rahn"), which gives guidelines for every aspect of life. Muslims must read a page of the Koran every day of the year and adhere to its teachings strictly. Only unswerving faith and the right conduct will ensure that they will go to heaven after death. This is achieved by following the five pillars of Islam. Muslims must also abstain from consuming pork and alcohol, and cannot have contact with dogs. For this reason there are no dogs in Maldives.

Maldivians belong to the Sunni sect, the largest sect in Islam. Although their faith is strong, it is quite liberal. Maldivians follow the teachings of the Koran but have not adopted the more extreme practices of Muslims in Saudi Arabia. For example women are not required to cover their faces with veils, and punishment does not involve violent physical retribution.

MALDIVIAN MOSQUES

Every island has a mosque for daily prayers, with separate sections for men and women. Male has more than 20 mosques, some of which are for women only. Most mosques are encircled by a peaceful garden with a well. Passers-by help themselves to the well water with long

ladles. The oldest mosque in Maldives is the Friday Mosque, dating from 1656. It has a beautiful interior with superb carvings.

PRAYER TIMES

Maldivians pray five times a day facing northwest in the direction of Mecca. The first prayer session of the day is in the first hour before sunrise, the second at around noon, the third in mid-afternoon, the fourth at sunset, and the last prayer is in the early evening. Muslims know they have to go to the mosque when they hear the call of the *muezzin* ("MOOD-zin") or mosque crier. In the old days the *muezzin* used to climb to the top of the minaret (a tower-like structure in the mosque) and shout out. Today mosques use a recording over loudspeakers on the minaret. The *muezzin* even appears on television. Shops and offices close for about 15 minutes after each call. Some people go to the mosque, while others spread out their prayer mats on the floor wherever they happen to be and kneel facing in the direction of Mecca.

Above: **Muslims are required to take off their shoes before entering a mosque.**

Opposite: **One of the newest mosques is the impressive Grand Friday Mosque situated in the Islamic Center. Its most striking feature is the golden dome glinting in the sun.**

The *nakaly* determines the best time for fishing, traveling, planting, building a house, or getting married in each two-week period.

THE ISLAMIC CALENDAR

Based on the cycles of the moon, the Islamic calendar started with the flight of Mohammed from Mecca in the year A.D. 622. That year marked year 1 of the Islamic calendar. Each year is composed of 12 months: Muharram, Safar, Rabi I, Rabi II, Jumada I, Jumada II, Rajab, Sha'ban, Ramadan, Shawwal, Dhu'l-Qa'dah, and Dhu'l-Hijja. As every month has only 30 days, the Islamic calendar moves faster than the Gregorian calendar used in most countries. It is for this reason that Muslim festivals and events do not fall on the same date every year. A new month starts on the evening when the new crescent moon is sighted.

All Maldivians refer to the Islamic calendar to mark personal events and dates. Those whose work deals with non-Muslims, however, also use the Gregorian calendar. In addition the islanders have devised their own calendar called *nakaly* ("NAH-kah-lih"). This calendar follows the changes in weather, the rising and setting of the stars, the sun, and the moon. The year is divided into 28 two-week periods.

SUPERSTITIONS

Despite being staunch Muslims, Maldivians are also very superstitious people. They believe in a number of spirits that inhabit the sea, the sky, the trees, and the rain. These spirits are called *dhevi* ("DAY-vi") in Dhivehi, or *jinnis* in Arabic. Although there are some helpful *dhevi*, most of them are malevolent. To keep them out, Maldivians sleep with all doors and windows tightly closed in spite of the heat. They also leave a kerosene lamp burning. Spirits help the islanders explain the forces of nature and any misfortune that befalls them. Maldivians do not see any conflict between their Islamic faith and their superstitions. Very often, they recite verses from the Koran in an attempt to ward off evil spirits.

Evidence of traditional worship.

DHEVI

One historian has counted more than 170 different *dhevi*. Their spiritual leader is Buddevi, who lives in jungles, on the beach, near thick undergrowth, or around abandoned houses. The Buddevi can take the shape of a cat or a man. It is said that whoever sees it will fall sick. Another spirit, Odivaru Ressi, lives in the sea and harms fishermen, boats, and fish. The lord of death is called Vigani. He inhabits the seas and can be seen on the water near the horizon. Appearing sometimes like a small man or a monkey with thick hair, he uses an elephant-like trunk to suck food from the graves of the dead. Vigani is the cause of sudden death and epidemics.

The people of the island of Gadhdhoo, which is located in the southern end of Maldives, believe in murderous giant cats that once invaded the neighboring island of Gan and killed all the inhabitants. For this reason they consider Gan to be unlucky and use it only as an Islamic cemetery. Although Gadhdhoo is heavily populated, no family would ever dream of moving to Gan.

WITCH DOCTORS

To neutralize evil spirits, islanders appeal to the *hakeem*, who is a witch doctor as well as a traditional medicine man. A combination of exorcist, conjurer, herbalist, and astrologer, the witch doctor is steeped in the art of *fandhita* ("FAN-dih-tah"). He becomes qualified to practice only after an arcane examination that is a mystery to most people. The witch doctor is most often called on when illness strikes, when a woman fails to conceive, or when the fishing catch is poor. He uses spells and lotions to cast out evil spirits. One remedy is to write phrases from the Koran on small strips of paper and stick them on the patient while reciting the sayings out loud.

Witch doctors cast spells primarily to heal or to encourage the elements to behave more favorably, like providing a better catch to fishermen. Other forms of good magic include making a sacred vow to perform good deeds if a wish is fulfilled. This may involve a sacrifice or the giving of alms. When a child is sick, bananas or a special pancake are distributed to neighbors and friends. The amount of food must be equal to the weight of the child. Black magic is also performed but very infrequently, and its practice may attract heavy punishment.

އަންހެނުންނަށް ދެވޭ އަނިޔާ

ޤުރުއާން

ނުރަނގަޅު ރަހުމު ކުޑަ އަމަލުތައް ހިންގުމަކީ ކުށެކެވެ

ޤުރުއާން ކިޔަވާ

LANGUAGE

THE OFFICIAL LANGUAGE OF MALDIVES is Dhivehi, a language that is unique to Maldives. Dhivehi is similar to other languages of the Indian subcontinent but is not based on any one of them. Many Maldivians also speak English, as it is an international business language and because the country used to be a British protectorate. English is the medium of instruction in grades 9 to 10 because students take the same qualifying exams as British schoolchildren. Now that tourism is becoming increasingly important as a sector of the economy, more Maldivians are learning English so that they can work in tourism-related businesses, which are paying relatively higher wages.

In addition to the two languages Dhivehi and English, Maldivian children also learn Arabic so that they can read the Koran. Those who are good in Arabic can go to the universities in the Middle East or Egypt.

Left: **A plank from the Old Friday Mosque with scriptures written in Arabic.**

Opposite: **Thaana, the script of Dhivehi, is used on this monument.**

Secondary school students listening intently in a class.

In addition to their Maldivian name, everybody also has an Arabic name. This is to enable them to make the *Haj*, or pilgrimage, to Mecca. When dealing with foreigners, they use their Arabic name.

Maldivians do not make use of much body language because they are a rather expressionless people. Conversations are carried on in a monotone. An onlooker would have no idea what is going on just from watching two Maldivians talking.

DHIVEHI

Dhivehi is closest to *Elu* ("AY-loo"), an ancient form of Sinhalese, the language of Sri Lanka. However, it has also borrowed words from Hindi, Arabic, English, and Bengali. Some language experts believe that the Maldivians first spoke Dhivehi as a form of secret code. As the ancient Maldivians traded mostly with Sri Lankans, they had to modify Sinhalese words or use them with different meanings so that the Sri Lankans would not understand what they were saying among themselves. It was also a way of defining their individuality as a nation so as not to be assimilated and invaded by the Sri Lankans or any other country. In Dhivehi the numbers from one to 12 are of Sinhalese origin, while the rest are Hindi. The names of the days are both Sinhalese and Hindi. Dhivehi has contributed one word to the English language—"atoll" from *atolhu*. The Maldivians are extremely proud of this.

Dhivehi is the language of the Maldivian administration. In the remoter islands it is the only language spoken by the inhabitants. Dhivehi has a number of dialects, particularly in the south, where the dialect has more similarities with Sinhalese. People in Male, for example, do not understand the dialect of Addu Atoll. Until the 1960s Dhivehi was the only medium of instruction in all schools. But today, with the growing need for further education, English is also taught.

A CLASS-CONSCIOUS LANGUAGE

Dhivehi is a class-conscious language. There are three classes. The highest level, called "nice language," is used to address members of the upper class and on national radio and television. The second level, which is less formal, is adopted to show respect for elders or to talk to government officials and strangers. Most Maldivians use informal Dhivehi, the third level, in everyday life.

Most young people are bilingual in English and Dhivehi.

MODERNIZING A LANGUAGE

For official correspondence with other countries and for the benefit of foreigners, the government introduced a Romanized transliteration of Maldivian names and words in 1977 in which the sounds are reproduced using the Roman alphabet. Words are spelled phonetically to produce something that looks familiar to the English-speaker. Many words, however, are mere approximations, and there is no correct or even consistent way of spelling local words in English language publications. For example, the word Dhivehi itself is sometimes spelled Divehi.

THE WRITTEN LANGUAGE

Dhivehi is written with a script called *Thaana* ("TAR-nah"). This script was invented by national hero Mohammed Thakurufaanu in the 16th century

Opposite: **A poster in the Thaana script.**

DHIVEHI PRONUNCIATION

In Dhivehi, stress always falls on the first syllable of the word. The language does not make use of difficult sounds; any English-speaker should be able to learn Dhivehi without having to learn new sounds. Consonants have the same sound as in English. Vowels are pronounced as follows:

a, as in "but"
aa, as in "rather"
ai, as in "cry"
e, as in "bed"
ee, as in "bee"
i, as in "grit"
o, as in "lot"
oa, as in "grow"
u, as in "put"

after he threw the Portuguese out of the country. *Thaana* consists of 24 letters, of which the first nine are forms of Arabic numerals. Vowels are written above the letters in the form of dashes. *Thaana* is written from right to left, which is similar to traditional Chinese script. Hence a Maldivian book actually starts on what we would consider the last page.

The earliest Dhivehi script was called *Evayla* ("AY-vay-lah"). It was written from left to right and contains many characters that are similar to Sinhalese. *Evayla* also included Arabic words. Another script, called *Dhives* ("DEE-vess"), replaced the *Evayla* in the 12th century. *Dhives* was also written from left to right. *Thaana*, which replaced *Dhives*, is written from right to left in order to accommodate the large number of Arabic words imported into Dhivehi. Similar in appearance to shorthand, *Thaana* looks like a series of tiger paw prints. It resembles Arabic but is fatter, with more squiggles. The oldest example of written Dhivehi is found on a series of ancient copper books called *Loamaafaanu* ("LOW-mar-far-noo"). The earliest book dates from 1195.

ENGLISH

Now the second language of most educated Maldivians, English was banned when the country gained independence. Although English has always been taught in Male, it was only taught in private schools, which very few Maldivians could afford. In the 1960s the government added English to the curriculum, making it compulsory for high school students to have a good knowledge of the language in order to pass their examinations.

Today many English words have been adopted into Dhivehi, in particular adjectives or attitudes that did not exist in traditional society. To turn an English word into Dhivehi, Maldivians attach the letter "u" at the end of the word, for instance, *dhoru* (door), *teacharu* (teacher), and *computaru* (computer).

GREETINGS

Maldivians may not appear to be very courteous to the casual observer because there are not many greeting words in Dhivehi. When meeting an acquaintance, the Maldivian either smiles or nods the head. Some men may shake hands, but only with other men, never with a woman. Physical closeness with a person of the opposite sex other than one's spouse is not allowed in Islam. Unlike most languages, where strangers or people one respects are greeted with the words "Mr.," "Mrs.," or "Ms.," the Maldivian language does not have such forms of address. Even when addressing a relative stranger, Maldivians will not use an honorific.

With the arrival of more foreigners in Maldives, Maldivian sophisticates now use the English "hello" to greet each other. It is less formal than the Arabic greeting *assalaamu alaikum* ("ASS-sahl-lar-moo ah-LAEE-koom"). Others use *kihineh* ("KEE-he-neh"), meaning "how?" Farewells are equally short. *Dhanee* ("DAH-nee"), which means "going," takes the place of good-bye. One recent introduction is *shukriyya* ("SHOE-kree-yah") for "thank you." Maldivians do not think it necessary to thank someone for a favor; they think the person doing the favor is only doing his or her duty.

NEWSPAPERS

Three daily newspapers are published in Maldives. Tabloid in format, they are between 14 and 16 pages long, with a few pages in English containing a useful digest of the day's main news from international agencies. *Haveeru*, the evening daily, enjoys the widest circulation. Mainly in Dhivehi, it has one or two pages in English. *Haveeru* does not appear on Fridays. The morning paper is called *Aafathis*, meaning "new morning." On Tuesdays it brings out a special English edition. Otherwise, only two pages daily are in English, including advertisements for movies. *Miadhu*, which means "today," comes out at noon everyday. The Maldivian government publishes a weekly newspaper in Dhivehi called *Furadhaana*. Young people read a monthly magazine, *Dhanfulhi*, with features in both Dhivehi and English. The only English-language publication is Mald*ives*

News Bulletin, a weekly issued by Maldives News Bureau of the Ministry of Information and Culture. It comes in four 8 by 11.5 inch (20 by 29 cm) pages.

RADIO AND TELEVISION

Voice of Maldives broadcasts throughout the archipelago for 11 hours every day. English-language news is read for 10 minutes in the early evening. TV Maldives, which started in 1978, is on the air from 10 A.M. to 11 P.M., with two breaks during the day. It broadcasts international news and entertainment programs consisting mainly of American soaps and cartoons. Local content seems more like community TV, with reports on school sports, religious and cultural events, news from the islands, and coverage of official appearances by the president and senior government leaders. Coverage is limited to a 19-mile (30-km) radius of Male.

Although censorship has eased considerably since President Gayoom came to power, the media are still strictly controlled. Open dissent against the government is not tolerated, and any publication that criticizes the government is immediately banned and its editors and writers banished or jailed.

ARTS

ALTHOUGH MALDIVIAN ARTS are not as spectacular as in India or Sri Lanka, local artists express themselves in a variety of ways with their limited raw materials. As Maldives is a Muslim country and reproduction of the human form is prohibited by Islam, there is no tradition of painting and sculpture. As many Maldivians do have a talent for design, however, many young people are producing contemporary graphic designs.

In the past some islands were famous for stone carving and the artists' talent can still be seen on old gravestones. The carving of calligraphy is also dying out. Old mosques display intricate calligraphy of the scriptures in both stone and wood. Today the Maldivian artistic feelings are seen more widely in arts and crafts. Local handicrafts, which once served a utilitarian purpose, are now produced for the tourist market.

LITERATURE

Maldives does not have much of a literary tradition, with its most prolific writers being Hassan Ahmed Maniku and President Gayoom. They have concentrated on the social, religious, economic, and historical aspects of the country. Maldives does have a rich oral tradition of myths and folk legends, but it is only recently that local folk tales have been published in Dhivehi and English. Most of them are stories of witchcraft and sorcery, while others preach against various sins and transgressions. It will take a few more decades for creative writing to find its place in Maldivian society.

Above: **Souvenir T-shirts for tourists are a creative outlet for young painters.**

Opposite: **An artisan patiently turning a pot.**

A worker carefully carves
intricate patterns on lacquerware.

LACQUERWARE

One of the most beautiful products by Maldivian artisans is lacquerware, wooden objects covered with colored resin. Traditionally, lacquered containers were presented as gifts to the sultan. These were mainly bowls, trays, and boxes of various sizes. Modern artisans have added vases, cups, and chess sets to their range. Nevertheless the designs still follow traditional colors and styles.

Many types of wood are used to produce lacquerware, although the traditional pieces are made from the local Alexandrian laurel. The whole process is done by hand, according to age-old practices. First the carver places a block of wood on a wheel that is turned by an assistant pulling a rope forward and backward around a spindle in a steady rhythm. As the wheel turns, the carver quickly chips at the wood with old-style tools to give it the desired shape. Next he uses sandpaper to smooth the object and then pours lacquer on it while the wheel is turned rapidly. Several colors of lacquer are applied in different layers, the craftsman waiting for each

LACQUERWARE FROM THULAADHOO

The best lacquerware comes from Thulaadhoo in Baa Atoll. Sitting informally in the shade of the island trees, a few elderly craftsmen keep alive a skill that has been passed down for generations. In the village square the posts holding up the platform where people meet are intricately covered in lacquer. Islanders love their lacquered plates and use them at religious and family festivals. The most impressive are large, round food boxes used to hold the family dinner on feast days. They have elaborately designed lids.

layer to harden before pouring on another color. Common colors are red, yellow, and green on a black background. Once all the layers have set, the carver uses a very sharp tool to make incisions into the various layers so as to produce a pattern. As he cuts away the lacquer, all the various colors appear as a motif. Most lacquered objects have abstract floral motifs with a close resemblance to Chinese artwork.

MALDIVIAN FURNITURE

Maldivians have invented two pieces of furniture that enable them to keep cool and relax. The *undhoali* ("OON-dow-lih") and *joli* ("JO-lih") are both used outdoors for sitting or reclining. When indoors, Maldivians sit and sleep on woven mats.

Undhoali is a type of swing that hangs on the verandah or from a tree in the garden. Made of a wooden platform hanging from an A-frame, it can seat several people. Sometimes called a bed-boat, the *undhoali* can be very elaborate, with a cot-like frieze at its ends and supports at the four corners. It is the perfect piece of furniture for taking a rest in the shade. A combination of sofa, hammock, and fan, the undhoali swings gently to lull its occupant to sleep, as the movement produces a slight breeze. Some villagers claim the movement of the *undhoali* reminds them of the gentle lapping waves.

Maldivian children enjoying themselves on the *joli*.

The *joli* has one of the same aims as the *undhoali*, that of cooling the occupant. It is a seat made of a rectangular frame with the sitting areas made of nets. It feels like sitting in a string shopping bag. The *joli* is divided into three or four sections to form individual, bucket-type seats. It is usually found outside the house, and strangers are welcome to sit down and take a rest while walking from one end of the island to the other.

ARCHITECTURE

Island houses are built of coral, a plentiful raw material in Maldives. Instead of using bricks, Maldivian builders use coral stones cemented to each other with lime. This lime is actually melted coral that is burned slowly in deep pits. Roofs are made of woven coconut leaves. Today more owners choose corrugated iron sheets to cover their houses.

Although iron roofs are hotter, they last longer than thatch. Village houses are not painted. They start out white because of the coral and take on a grayish tinge as time passes.

Houses are small with a few rooms, mainly meant for sleeping. Cooking is done in an outbuilding. The verandah and garden serve as the living areas. At the back is a well with a private courtyard. The walls surrounding this courtyard are high because the area around the well serves as an open-air bathroom. At road junctions the walls have rounded corners. This is a traditional feature that makes it easier for traffic to turn corners.

The most striking example of Maldivian architecture is the old Friday Mosque in Male. It was built in 1656 with coral stones that were fitted along grooves, not cemented with masonry. The interior is decorated with wood and coral carvings of local flora, and the roof contains 12 domes covered with bright designs in lacquer.

A typical Maldivian village. Every compound is enclosed by a chest-high coral wall.

Above: **The jewelers of Dhaal Atoll make the most delicate gold and silver chains, earrings, and bracelets.**

Opposite: **A skilled weaver making a** *cadjan.*

JEWELRY

On special occasions, Maldivian women wear intricately carved heavy silver bracelets and armlets, long thin belts that wrap several times around the waist, silver charm pendants, and gold necklaces. These have remained in the family for generations and point to the genius of the ancient jewelers. Although modern silversmiths and goldsmiths still produce outstanding jewelry, they cannot match their forefathers in brilliance. Most jewelers live in Dhaal Atoll, with goldsmiths on Ribudhoo and silversmiths on Hulhudheli. According to local belief, the sultan banished his chief jeweler to Ribudhoo after the latter was caught substituting gold-plated silver for the sultan's pure gold. The exiled artisan taught his skills to the islanders.

Coral and tortoiseshell jewelry is produced for the tourist market. Skilled craftsmen make beautiful necklaces and bracelets with fish bones decorated with black coral and mother-of-pearl. Although black coral is endangered, it is still fished in Lhaviyani Atoll. Local divers go to a depth of 98 feet (30 m) to harvest the beautiful brittle branches. When cut and polished, they are set into rings, earrings, pendants, and bangles.

WEAVING

The most common woven item is *cadjan* ("KAH-jan"), a mat made from coconut leaves sewn together with rope. It serves as roofing and as fencing. *Cadjan* mats are also used for sleeping and to line seats. The finest mat in Maldives is the *kuna* ("KOO-nah"). It can be as small as a place mat or as large as a mattress. It is a specialty of the women of Huvadhoo Atoll who only use the reeds from their own islands. Collecting the reeds, drying them, and weaving a mat can take weeks. It is mostly a labor of love because the mats do not fetch a very high price in the shops. The reeds are dried in the sun and stained with natural dyes. Colors are muted, ranging from fawn to black. When the reeds are ready, they are woven into intricate abstract designs on a wooden loom. Some women weave on a rope frame pegged out to hold the warp.

Few people still weave textiles, but Eydhafushi in Baa Atoll was once famous for its *feyli* ("FAY-lih"), a heavy white cotton sarong with brown and black strands. Many old women still wear the *feyli* as an underskirt.

LEISURE

LIFE IN THE ISLANDS is sometimes quite harsh, so for most people, leisure means resting in the shade and enjoying the cool breeze. While the men gather in the village square for a chat in the late afternoon, the women usually get together during the day when they sweep the streets or clean the beaches. Families swing gently on the *undhaoli* or sit on the *joli* while talking to neighbors or friends. Many old women like to smoke the *guda-guda* ("GOO-dah GOO-dah"), a waterpipe that makes a gurgling sound, hence the local name. Sitting on a mat, the smoker places the round bottle of water on the ground next to her feet. Two metal tubes are inserted into the lid, one linking the bottle to the tobacco burning in a funnel and the other to a long rubber hose. To smoke, she brings the hose to her mouth and inhales the smoke. Many men also like to indulge in conventional cigarette smoking.

Left: **A woman enjoys a smoke on the *guda-guda*.**

Opposite: **Boys playing on a boat.**

Above: **Playing beach volleyball. Maldivians enjoy sports, especially ball games. However, most participants are male.**

Opposite: **A young boy about to set off for a casual game of soccer with his friends.**

SPORTS

Although most foreigners go to Maldives for watersports, especially diving, Maldivians do not look to the sea for recreation. Only young children play in the sea. They do so fully clothed as dictated by Islamic modesty. Older children do not swim because wearing wet clothes that cling to the body is improper. As is to be expected from a former British protectorate, the two most popular sports in Maldives are soccer and cricket, two typically British games.

CRICKET Similar to baseball, cricket is played on an oval grass field by two teams of 11 players each taking turns to bowl at a wicket defended by a batter from the opposing team. Players are dressed in long-sleeved white shirts and trousers, and batters wear shin pads to protect their legs. President Gayoom is a keen cricket player, and his enthusiasm has helped to popularize the game. The season starts in March, and many teams take part in the national tournament.

SOCCER is, without doubt, the national sport of Maldives. Every island has a soccer field where young men gather for an informal match in the late afternoon. On Male alone, there are more than 30 teams playing in the semi-professional national soccer league. The teams are divided into three divisions, and important games are played at the National Stadium. Three main tournaments pit the teams against each other every year. Foreign teams, usually from Sri Lanka, are invited to participate in the President of Maldives Invitation Soccer Cup. Soccer fans who do not live in Male can join in the action "live" through radio and television broadcasts of the main matches. The inter-atoll championship is a big affair, with the entire island, including women and children, turning out for the final. After the game, everybody takes part in a big feast that sprawls out into the streets. A veritable soccer fever grips the entire nation every four years during the soccer World Cup. Soccer is the only sport where Maldives has been able to defeat foreign teams.

TRADITIONAL SPORTS

Bashi ("BAH-shi") is an ancient Maldivian game that is popular throughout the islands. Only girls play this sport. In Male young women enjoy a game of *bashi* in the parks in the early evening. Played on a kind of tennis court with a net separating the teams, the game consists of bashing a ball over the net while facing away from the opponents. The girls in the opposing team try to catch the ball with their hands. Each team consists of about 11 players. The game derives its name from the hand-woven *bashi*. The *bashi* is a kind of bat made from coconut palm leaves and traditionally used to hit the ball. Today, however, most girls use a tennis racket and ball. Although *bashi* is played everywhere, there is no tournament.

Another ancient game is *thin mugoali* ("THIN MOO-go-lih"), which has been played in the atolls for more than 400 years. This game is very similar to baseball. The objective is to make as many home runs as possible. The base consists of a circle made by rotating on one foot in the sand. The sun-hardened lower part of a coconut leaf stem serves as the bat, and the squarish ball is made of coconut fronds.

Mandi ("MAHN-dee") is a type of primitive lacrosse. The players use long sticks to hurl and catch a small stick without letting it drop on the ground. Young men also like to engage in *bai bala* ("BY BAH-lah"), a Maldivian form of tag wrestling. The player enters a ring and tries to touch the members of the opposite team. If he is not pulled out of the ring by an opponent, the person he has touched is eliminated.

Two men playing chess. When making a move, the player bangs the piece down hard.

BOARD GAMES

People in Maldives like to play board games because they are not physically demanding and can be played in the cool shade of a large tree. Chess is a favorite game with older men, who play it fast and with great gusto. However, this is a modified version of the classic game with different rules. Maldivian chess sets, consisting of lacquered chess pieces, are made locally. The chess pieces are yellow and red and shaped like divots; only the size distinguishes one from the other.

Carrom ("KAH-rom"), an Arabic game also popular in India and Sri Lanka, is played by younger people, since it involves more dexterity and hand-eye coordination. A form of pool, it uses a large board with pockets in the four corners. Players face each other and shove a flat disc with their forefingers to try and push smaller black or white discs into the pockets. The first one to pocket all his or her discs wins the game. Four persons can play carrom in teams of two, with team members facing each other.

Younger children play *ovvalhu* ("OH-vah-loo"). The board is carved out of a wooden block and has 16 little depressions. Cowry shells are placed in the depressions. It is a good way of teaching children how to count.

LEISURE IN MALE

People in Male have more facilities for leisure. Apart from traditional sports and board games, they can watch television or go to the movies. Two theaters screen movies from India and Hollywood, with all sexy scenes snipped out by the censors' scissors. Three-hour Hindi epics produced by the studios in Bombay are very popular among Maldivians because they include songs, dances, and drama. American movies are shown in English.

Many residents of Male like to take a stroll in the cool evening air. Sometimes they hang out at teashops or play *carrom* or chess. Concerts and exhibitions are an occasional treat.

A video shop in Male. Maldivians like action-packed thrillers.

Girls beating pot drums and dancing.

SONG AND DANCE

Despite their Islamic upbringing, Maldivians show little restraint in their songs and dances. It is in their dances that Maldivians express their repressed emotions and acknowledge their varied ancestry. African, Indian, and Arabian influences can be seen in their songs and dance. Traditional songs and dances have not changed over the centuries.

Dances are usually performed to celebrate special occasions and are ritualized around specific ceremonies and rites of passage such as circumcision. Men and women have separate dances that reflect their different activities. Accompaniment is provided mainly by drums, tambourines, bells, and scrapers. Drums are made from a hollowed coconut trunk covered with the skin of a ray or the stomach lining of a shark. Musicians are usually male, especially drummers, but women have taken to beating pot drums in recent years. The songs that accompany the dance sometimes tell a story if they are in Dhivehi or are just a string of unintelligible sounds, including some African and Arabic words.

Girls beating pot drums and dancing.

FEMALE DANCES

Women mainly take part in three dances: *maafathi neshun* ("MAR-fah-tee NAY-shoon"), *bandiya jehun* ("BAN-dih-yah JAY-hoon"), and *bolimalaafath neshun* ("BOH-lih-mah-lar-fat NAY-shoon"). *Maafathi neshun* is a festival dance performed in national dress. Two rows of 10 women carry bows with artificial flowers attached to them. They are accompanied by three drummers and singers, who sing songs that express national feelings and are set to Indian music. *Bandiya jehun* is a harvest and fertility dance similar to the Indian pot dance. The dancers set the rhythm by beating on the metal water pots they carry. To make a louder

Professional dancers in a colorful performance.

sound, they wear metal rings on their fingers. The dance is performed in both standing and seated positions. The most important of all women's dances, the *bolimalaafath neshun* originates from the tradition of offering gifts to the sultan. The gift is in the form of shells contained in a small box or vase covered with a bright silk cloth. Twenty-four women, dressed in brightly colored local costumes infused with the scent of burning incense, are required for this dance. As they sing and dance, they form into groups of two, three, or four and walk toward the sultan to offer him the gift.

MALE DANCES

A male dance in which it is the sultan's turn to offer gifts to the people is *gaa odi lava* ("GAR OH-dih LAH-vah"). Each dancer carries a stick, and they slowly walk in two rows toward a box containing the gift. While still dancing and singing, they form a circle around the box before taking it away. The rhythm increases as the song and dance progress. *Dhandi jehun* ("DAN-dih JAY-hoon") is a stick dance performed differently from atoll to atoll. Facing a partner, each dancer holds a stick about 3 feet (90 cm) long. As he dances, he strikes his stick on the one belonging to his partner. The rhythm is provided by the beating sticks, and the men sing along as they dance. A variation of this dance is the *jehun* ("JAY-hoon"), which is performed seated. As they strike their sticks, the dancers show off their skill by twisting and gyrating their torsos to the music. *Thaara* ("TAR-rah") is a semireligious song performed in Arabic in fulfillment of a vow. The most common dance is *bodu beru* ("BOW-doo BAY-roo"), thought to have been introduced to Maldives by Africans in the 12th century. Swaying to the rhythm of loud drums and clapping, dancers leap and jerk as if in a trance, striking almost grotesque poses. *Bodu beru* is usually performed after a hard day's work.

The lyrics of the Bodu beru *have no meaning because they consist of a mixture of* Dhivehi, African, *and other words.*

FESTIVALS

MALDIVIANS CELEBRATE TWO TYPES OF HOLIDAYS: national days with a historical significance and religious festivals. All celebrations are community affairs as men, women, and children share in the preparation of food, decorations, and entertainment. Contrary to most Muslim countries, many religious holidays in Maldives are celebrated over several days of feasting, dancing, and merrymaking. Most festivals involve a blend of the modern with the traditional. Folk dances accompanied by traditional instruments can be followed by pop songs. Some villages put on a performance of pot dancers or a *raivaru* recital. All celebrations usually end with a *bodu beru*, the energetic Maldivian dance with an irresistible beat.

Left: A festival celebration along the waterfront in Male.

Opposite: Dressed in their best clothes, these Maldivians are waiting for the Kuda Id parade to begin.

KUDA ID

The most important festival in Maldives is Kuda Id, which marks the end of Ramadan, the Islamic fasting month. For one whole month, everyone fasts from sunrise to sunset. The only exception are very young children or the physically frail. This is a real test of faith as the climate of Maldives makes it very difficult to go without water for one whole day. In addition Muslims are supposed to abstain from sex and other pleasures, such as smoking, during the month.

As the sun sets, a horn shell is sounded to tell people that they can break their fast. Islanders rush to drink coconut milk or tea and eat some snacks while waiting for their dinner of rice and fish curry. Ramadan food is specially prepared to restore the energy lost during the day. Those fasting will wake up before dawn the next day to eat a meal of rice and fish sauce.

THE NEW MOON

On the 30th day of Ramadan religious scholars go to sea in a boat to witness the birth of the new moon, which signals the end of the fasting month. The next day is Kuda Id. If they do not see the new crescent, the people carry on fasting one more day until it is confirmed that the new moon has risen. A cannon announces the end of Ramadan in Male.

Maldivians celebrate Kuda Id for three days. The first day starts with a prayer, followed by a special lunch to which family and friends are invited. Children ask their elders for forgiveness, and the whole festival is characterized by a sense of family togetherness. Food and money are given to charity, and everyone exchanges greeting cards. In the afternoon they put on their new clothes for the Id parade. The main streets are filled with colorful bands and marchers.

Faithful Muslims are treated to a long-awaited sumptuous spread at the end of Ramadan.

OTHER RELIGIOUS FESTIVALS

Two lunar months and 10 days after Kuda Id, Maldivians celebrate Bodu Id to mark the *Haj* pilgrimage to the Muslim holy city of Mecca in Saudi Arabia. All Muslims try to go on the *Haj* once in their lifetime for an uplifting spiritual experience. Bodu Id is four days of solid feasting and celebration. People say special prayers and play Bodu Id games. On some islands residents splash each other with water. Many also visit other islands to enjoy the festivities.

Prophet Mohammed's Birthday is another Muslim holiday that is celebrated with great gusto. For three whole days families invite one another to share their food in villages throughout the islands.

During the period of the Haj, the airport is thronged by masses of people sending off or welcoming back their relatives.

PATRIOTISM

Maldivians have a strong sense of national pride; they commemorate all occasions in their history when the nation has triumphed over attempts to curb their sovereignty. All national holidays are celebrated with parades, and various organizations participate in the marching bands. Elaborate fireworks decorate the night sky as the older generation recount the struggle for independence. In the villages, children have their own parade. Smartly dressed, they march through the main street watched by their proud parents, neighbors, and other spectators. Houses are decorated with the national flag, and some patriotic young men even paint themselves green and red.

A National Day celebration.

A school marching band takes part in the National Day parade.

NATIONAL HOLIDAYS

National Day is celebrated on the first day of the third lunar month. It commemorates the end of the Portuguese occupation in 1578. Also associated with the Portuguese occupation is Martyr's Day, which marks the death of Sultan Ali VI at the hands of the Portuguese invaders in 1558. Huravee Day celebrates the overthrow of the Malabars of India who occupied Maldives for a few months in 1752. Independence Day, which marks the end of the British Protectorate in 1965, is celebrated on July 26 every year. Republic Day commemorates the founding of the second republic in 1968 and is celebrated in Male with brass band performances and parades. Victory Day falls on November 3. Maldivians celebrate their victory over the Tamil mercenaries from Sri Lanka, who tried to overthrow the government in 1988.

In keeping with the Maldivian zest for festivals, most national holidays last at least two days. The actual day is devoted to official parades while the next day is for the people to enjoy themselves.

BIRTH AND DEATH

A newborn baby receives its name on the seventh day after its birth. During the ceremony, a special prayer is said, and food is given to the poor. On many islands the parents also shave the baby's head for this occasion. Birthdays are not usually celebrated nor even remembered. On a person's death, the burial takes place within 24 hours. The family offers a special prayer followed by a feast on the 40th day after the death.

A married couple with their newborn child. Similar to birthdays, marriages are simple ceremonies where the bride does not even need to be present.

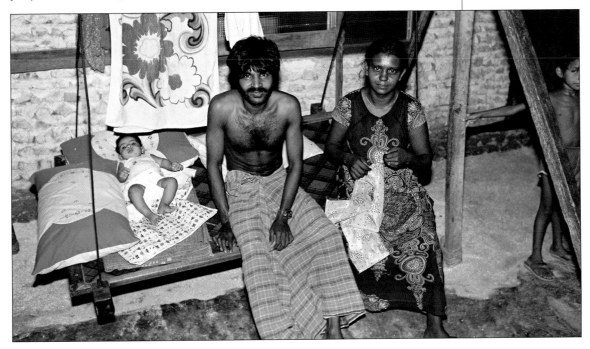

THE RITE OF CIRCUMCISION

The most important rite of passage for boys is circumcision. Mandated by Islam, it is performed when a boy turns 6 and involves snipping off the foreskin of the sexual organ. Circumcision usually takes place during the December school vacations, and several families get together to defray the cost. While the boys are being circumcised, their relatives massage their feet and sing and dance to take their minds off the pain. They take about three days to recover. Throughout the three days, sometimes for one week, the families organize a big party with plenty of entertainment and food. The house is decorated with colorful bright lights, and guests will bring beautiful presents for the boys.

Friends and family celebrate the circumcision of a young boy with dance and song, and plenty of good food.

CALENDAR OF FESTIVALS

Holidays that have a fixed date every year are:
New Year's Day : January 1
Independence Day : July 26
Victory Day : November 3
Republic Day : November 11
Fishermen's Day : December 10

Holidays that follow the Islamic lunar calendar are:
Islamic New Year
National Day
Prophet Mohammed's Birthday
Huravee Day
Martyr's Day
Kuda Id
Bodu Id

On the islands, it is the medicine man that is in charge of circumcision; children in Male are taken to a doctor.

FOOD

AS IN OTHER ASPECTS OF LIFE, Maldivian cuisine is the result of various foreign influences. Most dishes tend to be spicy, with curry being a firm favorite. A feature of the Maldivian diet is the lack of green vegetables and fresh fruits. The vegetables and fruit available in the markets are expensive because most of them are imported.

The Maldivian family eats three full meals a day: breakfast, lunch, and dinner. In between they snack on a variety of sweets and other treats. Maldivians eat with their right hand, rolling the food into a ball and pushing it into the mouth with the thumb. Some Male residents now use a spoon.

Maldivians enjoy chewing on betel leaves after a meal. This custom, which is a few centuries old, is supposed to aid digestion and freshen the breath. It also acts as a mild stimulant. Maldivians start the habit when young. From the age of 14, men and women chew little packets of betel leaves wrapped around areca nut and lime during the day. For this reason Maldivians usually have teeth stained dark by the red betel juice.

FISH AND COCONUT

Two ingredients predominate in the Maldivian diet: fish and coconut. These two products are plentiful in the country. Fish, usually tuna, is eaten in all its forms: fresh, dried, salted, smoked, or canned. Maldivians even have a fish paste that they spread on bread or mix with rice. They also use the fish paste as a dip for cut fruit. All meals, including breakfast, will include the main staples of fish, rice, and coconut.

Above: **A vendor preparing to sell betel in an indoor market.**

Opposite: **Selling local produce in an outdoor market.**

Apart from fish, Maldivians eat very little other meat. Chicken is a real treat and is reserved for special occasions, such as Kuda Id or a circumcision feast. It is usually cooked in curry. Another special treat is *biryani* ("BEER-yah-nih"), rice cooked with fragrant spices, meat, and potatoes.

CARBOHYDRATES

The main source of carbohydrate for Maldivians is rice. Usually steamed, it is sometimes cooked with coconut milk and chili. As importing rice drains precious foreign exchange, the government is encouraging the population to turn to other starchy foods, especially breadfruit, which grows well in the islands. It is usually cut into thin slices and fried for a snack. Breadfruit curry, called *babukeylu hithi* ("BAH-boo-kay-loo HEE-tih"), is very popular on some islands. Other locally grown starchy vegetables include taro and sweet potatoes. *Roshi* ("ROE-shi") is a type of bread made from flour, water, oil, and salt, and is usually eaten for breakfast.

THE NATIONAL DISH

The national dish is *garudhiya* ("GAH-roo-dya"), a pungent treacle-like soup with chunks of fresh tuna in it. Maldivians smother their rice with it and accompany the meal with lime juice, chili, and onions. Fish is also fried and cooked in curries. For dry fish curry, small pieces of fresh fish are fried in many spices. Smoked fish is usually eaten for breakfast. It is mixed with coconut, onions, chili, and lime juice, and eaten with *roshi*.

Maldivian men gathered at the fish market in the late afternoon to buy fresh catch.

THE WATER PROBLEM

Ironically, for a country surrounded by water, Maldives has severe water problems. As the islands are flat, the country has no natural reservoirs at ground level. Rainwater collects at around 6 feet (2 m) underground, and Maldivians draw their fresh water from wells. Sometimes they have to line up for a long time with their pails, awaiting their turn. However, if more water is drawn than supplied by rains, seawater infiltrates the ground and mixes with the fresh water. The water table in Male was dangerously low when the government decided to build desalination plants.

Today Male residents get fresh water piped to their homes. Four desalination plants built with the help of the Danish and French governments produce enough water for the needs of the island. Resort islands also have their own small desalination plants. Through the process of reverse osmosis, seawater is distilled into pure drinking water. These plants consist of racks of metal cylinders, each containing an inner cylinder made of a polymer membrane. Seawater is pumped into the inner cylinder at high pressure and the membrane allows the pure water to flow to the outer cylinder from where it is piped away. The Coca-Cola plant in North Male is the only one in the world to use seawater to manufacture its drink—after it has been desalinated, of course.

The other islands have devised their own ways to collect rainwater. Large reservoirs are built on the roofs of schools and mosques, and the islanders collect their fresh water from a tap.

While women and chil-
dren in the islands spend
a lot of time collecting
firewood for cooking,
Male residents buy theirs
from the firewood mar-
ket.

FOOD PREPARATION

Maldivian women do their cooking in a separate building away from the main house. This is to prevent smoke from getting into the living and sleeping quarters. Although some houses in Male have gas or even electric stoves, most households still use wood-burning stoves. Stoves are placed on the ground, and Maldivian women squat down to do their cooking.

The coconut grater is an important utensil as all coconut used in cooking is always freshly grated. The grater is actually a low stool with a sharp jagged blade fixed at one end. The coconut is split in two and the meat is grated on the jagged blade. The grated coconut collects on a tray placed underneath the blade. When a woman does the grating, she sits sidesaddle on the stool. If it is a man, he straddles the stool.

Maldivian women spend a lot of time preparing food. Rice has to be husked in large trays and stones and seeds discarded. To make coconut honey, they have to grate the coconuts, collect the coconut milk, and stir the pot over the fire for several hours.

MARKETS

Villages do not have markets. In Male, however, the markets along the waterfront are a hive of activity. The most interesting is the fish market. In the late afternoon, when the fishing *dhoni* return, men rush to unload the fat tuna, bonito, and swordfish and carry them across the road into an open-sided area with a tiled floor. The fish are immediately gutted and cleaned. They are sold on the spot and taken home in carts or hanging from a bicycle's handlebars. The fish market is kept spotless by daily washing and disinfecting.

Next to the fish market stands the produce market. Located in a covered building, it sells a limited range of fruits and vegetables, rice, coconuts,

Selling coconuts and bananas in a produce market.

eggs, and toddy. The atmosphere is peaceful inside the market as vendors wait quietly for customers to approach them. In the open space in front of the produce market, firewood is sold, including coconut and screwpine wood brought in by *dhoni* from neighboring islands. The vendors are joined by others selling watches, ladles, and underwear.

SHORT EATS

Maldivians are very fond of eating snacks that they call "short eats." (A meal with rice and curry is called a "long eat.") These are like finger foods or cakes. Short eats can be either sweet or savory. Sweets are made from flour, sugar, coconut, and eggs. Savories are based on a mixture of dried smoked

Maldivian men enjoying their afternoon tea. Custards and puddings are popular sweet snacks for tea.

The village tea bar is the place villagers go for tea and simple snacks.

fish, grated coconut, lime juice, onion, and chili. Savories are usually small and brown while sweets are light or brightly colored. Short eats are washed down with tea.

Gula ("GOO-lah") is a favorite short eat. Smoked fish mixed with coconut, onion, ginger, and chili is rolled into a ball and wrapped in pastry, then fried. *Kuli bokibaa* ("KOO-lih BOH-kih-bar") is made from soaked rice, smoked fish, onion, ginger, chili, and coconut. The mixture is kneaded, baked in a tin, and cut into squares before serving. The Maldivian version of the samosa is called *bajiyaa* ("BAH-jia"). This fried pastry triangle is stuffed with canned tuna, onion, chili, and lemon grass.

Foni bokibaa ("FOH-nee BOH-kih-bah") is a pudding made from rice flour, coconut, water, sugar, and rose water. It is baked and cut into squares. *Huni foli* ("HOO-nee FOH-lih") is *roshi* stuffed with a paste of coconut, honey, and water. It is rolled up like a burrito and fried.

A typical teashop. The men, although strangers to one another, are sharing a table.

EATING OUT

Most Maldivians do not entertain at home. They prefer to take their guests to a restaurant for a meal. When dining out, the host always pays. It is very bad manners for a guest to reach for the bill and offer to pay. When they have no guests to entertain, few families eat out.

The teashop is the most common place to eat in Maldives. Frequented by men only, it is a type of cafe that serves short eats and tea. It does not have a menu because all the food is either already set out on the tables or brought by the waiter without the diner having to ask for it. The customer helps himself to whatever he fancies and pays for only what he has eaten. As the tables are shared by several persons, it is not easy for the waiter to keep track of what one person has consumed. Teashops open at 5 A.M. and close in the evening. The popular ones don't shut their doors until 1 A.M. However none of them is open 24 hours. The teashop offers the best opportunity for Maldivian men from all walks of life to socialize and meet friends.

DRINKS

Most islanders drink plain water of course. To wash down their short eats, they drink sweetened hot tea. In Male, Maldivians can choose from a range of soft drinks manufactured locally. Coca-Cola and bitter lemon are very popular. *Suji* ("SOO-jih"), a local drink made with semolina, coconut milk, nuts, raisins, and a dash of spices, is a refreshing drink. A favorite local drink is toddy. This is the nectar tapped from the crown of the coconut palm at the point where the coconuts grow. Toddy is sweet and natural and tastes better than it smells. The cloudy liquid can be drunk immediately after it has been tapped, and that is how Maldivians like it. If it is left for a while, the sugar starts to ferment, and it becomes slightly alcoholic. Every island has a toddy tapper. However, toddy is becoming scarcer now because young people do not want to become toddy tappers. They see it as a socially humble job.

HOW TO MAKE BARABO PIRINEE

5 cups pumpkin, grated
1 cup yellow raisins
$^1/_2$ cup flour
1 cup chopped nuts
1 cup water
1 can condensed milk
Vanilla flavoring to taste

Boil water in a pan. Add pumpkin and cook until soft.
Stir in raisins and cook on low heat for a couple of minutes.
Add milk, vanilla flavoring, and nuts. Stir well.
Mix flour with a little water and add to the pumpkin mixture. Cook until thick and consistent.
Serve the pudding warm or chilled.

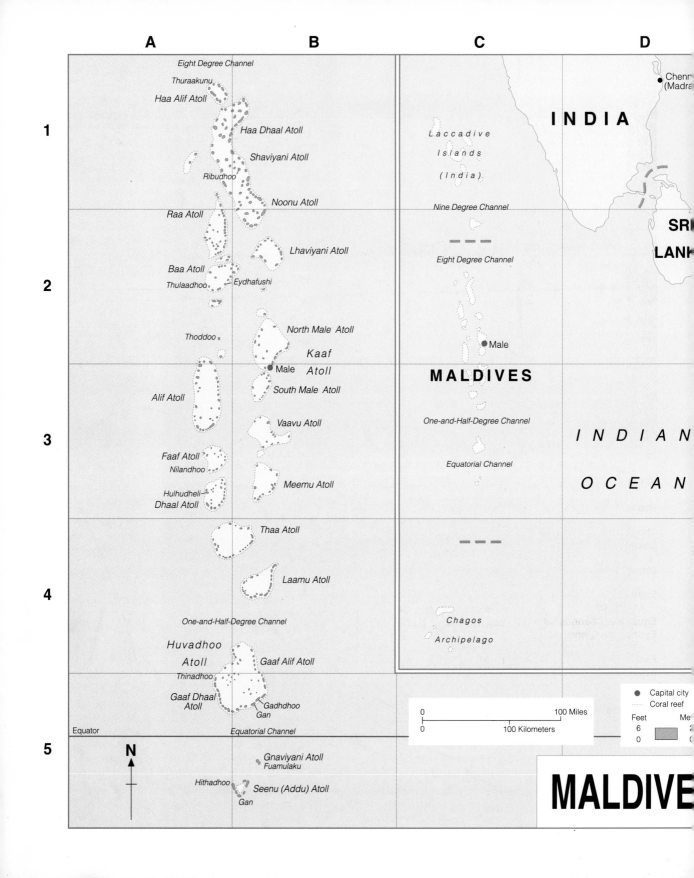

	A	B	C	D

1

Eight Degree Channel

Thuraakunu

Haa Alif Atoll

Haa Dhaal Atoll

Shaviyani Atoll

Ribudhoo

Noonu Atoll

Raa Atoll

2

Lhaviyani Atoll

Baa Atoll

Thulaadhoo · Eydhafushi

North Male Atoll

Thoddoo

Kaaf

Male *Atoll*

South Male Atoll

Alif Atoll

3

Vaavu Atoll

Faaf Atoll

Nilandhoo

Hulhudheli

Meemu Atoll

Dhaal Atoll

Thaa Atoll

Laamu Atoll

4

One-and-Half-Degree Channel

Huvadhoo

Atoll

Gaaf Alif Atoll

Thinadhoo

Gaaf Dhaal

Atoll

Gadhdhoo

Gan

Equator

Equatorial Channel

5

N

Gnaviyani Atoll

Fuamulaku

Hithadhoo · Seenu (Addu) Atoll

Gan

INDIA

Chenn
(Madra

Laccadive

Islands

(India)

Nine Degree Channel

Eight Degree Channel

Male

MALDIVES

One-and-Half-Degree Channel

Equatorial Channel

Chagos

Archipelago

SR

LANK

INDIAN

OCEAN

0	100 Miles
0	100 Kilometers

● Capital city
----- Coral reef

Feet   Me
6   2
0   0

MALDIVE

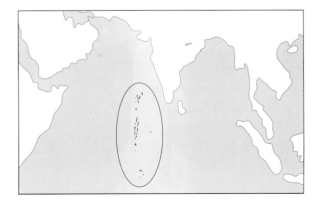

QUICK NOTES

OFFICIAL NAME
Dhivehi Raajjeyge Jumhuriyya or Republic of Maldives

NATIONAL FLAG
A green rectangle surrounded by a red border, with a white crescent in the center.

CLIMATE
Tropical

TOTAL AREA
34,750 square miles (90,003 square km), of which 115 square miles (298 square km) is land

NUMBER OF ISLANDS
1,190

CAPITAL
Male

ADMINISTRATIVE ATOLLS
Alif, Baa, Dhaal, Faaf, Gaaf Alif, Gaaf Dhaal, Gnaviyani, Haa Alif, Haa Dhaal, Kaafu, Laamu, Lhaviyani, Meemu, Noonu, Raa, Seenu, Shaviyani, Thaa, Vaavu

FAMOUS LEADERS
Sultan Mohamed Ibn Abdulla
Mohamed Thakurufaanu
Hassan Manifukaan
Mohammed Amin Didi
Maumoon Abdul Gayoom

POPULATION
300,220 (July 1999 estimate)

OFFICIAL LANGUAGE
Dhivehi

OFFICIAL RELIGION
Islam

NATIONAL FLOWER AND TREE
Pink rose and coconut palm

CURRENCY
1 rufiyaa = 100 laari
US$1 = Rf11.85

MAIN EXPORTS
Fish, clothes, scrap metal

MAJOR IMPORTS
Food, petroleum products, machinery, consumer goods

MAIN TRADING PARTNERS
Singapore, India, Malaysia, Sri Lanka, United Kingdom, Japan, United States, Germany

ANNIVERSARIES
Independence Day (July 26)
Victory Day (November 3)
Republic Day (November 11)
Huravee Day
Martyr's Day

GLOSSARY

atolhu varin ("AH-toh-loo VAH-rin")
The administrator for an atoll.

bandiya jehun ("BAN-dih-yah JAY-hoon")
Pot dance performed by very young women.

bodu beru ("BOW-doo BAY-roo")
Energetic dance performed by men on special occasions or after a hard day's work.

circumcision
Removing the foreskin of the male sexual organ.

dhevi ("DAY-vi")
Spirits that live in objects such as the sky, the trees, or the sea.

Dhives ("DEE-vess")
A written form of the Maldivian language.

dhoni ("DOE-nih")
A wooden boat with a distinctive curved prow used for fishing and transportation.

feyli ("FAY-lih")
A heavy white cotton sarong with brown and black strands.

ghaazee ("HAR-zee")
A religious leader.

gula ("GOO-lah")
A fish ball wrapped in pastry and fried.

Haj ("HAJJ")
The pilgrimage to Mecca that should be done at least once in the lifetime of every Muslim.

hakeem ("HAH-keem")
A traditional medicine man or woman.

joli ("JO-lih")
A seat made of a wooden frame with a net.

Majlis ("MADGE-liss")
Government assembly.

nakaly ("NAH-kah-lih")
A calendar based on the changes in weather, the rising and setting of the stars, the sun, and the moon.

Ramadan
The Muslim fasting month when no food or drink can be consumed from sunrise to sunset.

Redin
A mythical light-skinned people who worshiped the sun. They are thought to be the original inhabitants of Maldives.

Thaana ("TAR-nah")
The written script of the Maldivian language.

undhoali ("OON-dow-lih")
A type of outdoor swing used for sitting and sleeping.

BIBLIOGRAPHY

Anderson, Charles and Hasiz, Ahamed. *Common Fish of the Maldives*. Male: Novelty, 1987.

Gayoom, Maumoon Abdul. *The Maldives: A Nation in Peril*. Republic of Maldives: Ministry of Planning, Human Resources and Environment, 1998.

Hooper, Neil. *Maldives (Let's Visit Places and Peoples of the World)*. New York: Chelsea House, 1989.

INDEX

INDEX

INDEX